RETIRE
FREE

RETIRE FREE

FIVE STEPS TOWARD LIVING
YOUR BEST RETIREMENT

ROBERT A. GUY, RICP®

Published by Advantage, Charleston, South Carolina.
Member of Advantage Media Group.

ADVANTAGE is a registered trademark, and the Advantage colophon is a trademark of Advantage Media Group, Inc.

Printed in the United States of America.

10 9 8 7 6 5 4 3 2 1

ISBN: 978-1-59932-424-1
LCCN: 2019930592

Cover design by Melanie Cloth.
Layout design by Carly Blake.

This publication is designed to provide accurate and authoritative information in regard to the subject matter covered. It is sold with the understanding that the publisher is not engaged in rendering legal, accounting, or other professional services. If legal advice or other expert assistance is required, the services of a competent professional person should be sought.

 Advantage Media Group is proud to be a part of the Tree Neutral® program. Tree Neutral offsets the number of trees consumed in the production and printing of this book by taking proactive steps such as planting trees in direct proportion to the number of trees used to print books. To learn more about Tree Neutral, please visit www.treeneutral.com.

Advantage Media Group is a publisher of business, self-improvement, and professional development books and online learning. We help entrepreneurs, business leaders, and professionals share their Stories, Passion, and Knowledge to help others Learn & Grow. Do you have a manuscript or book idea that you would like us to consider for publishing? Please visit advantagefamily.com or call 1.866.775.1696.

To Mum and Dad

Table of Contents

Preface

In 1979, my father made a comment at the dinner table that changed the course of my life. He was a former Marine drill instructor and a Korean War combat veteran. As you might imagine, when he spoke, I listened.

After the war, he began a career in financial services. I remember one evening at dinner my mom asking him how his day went. With a big smile and great enthusiasm, my dad told us how a client had called him that afternoon to thank him for the advice my dad had given him over the years. The man told him this advice helped him and his family feel "tremendous peace of mind and sense of security" regarding his recent retirement. My dad went on to explain that this gentleman had worked very hard his whole life to provide for his family, and now, because of the advice my dad had given him, he was going to be able to enjoy his retirement years with no reduction in lifestyle and no fear of running out of money.

My dad used this opportunity to teach his four children a very valuable lesson. He told us: "The key to finding happiness and fulfillment in life is to help other people get what they want. If you only try to get what *you* want, you will end up being miserable and unfulfilled.

Helping others is the secret to true satisfaction and happiness in life."

Those words had a profound impact on me. Even though I was only a sophomore in high school, I made the decision right then and there to follow in my dad's footsteps. It seemed like the perfect profession to practice what he was preaching. If I could help others find security, comfort, and peace of mind in their financial lives, then I would be able to attain those same feelings for myself. I immediately began learning everything I could about finance, economics, markets, investments, and taxes. Not many of my friends were reading the *Wall Street Journal* at fifteen years old, but I had found something I was truly passionate about.

In 1988, I graduated from the University of Massachusetts Isenberg School of Management with a bachelor of science degree in business and finance. After graduation, I immediately began a career in the field I had already been studying for years. I've been a professional financial advisor for more than twenty-five years now and have not lost my desire to help people retire successfully.

I decided to write this book because over the last several years I have noticed that it has become more and more difficult for people to achieve any type of financial security in retirement. It seems like there is more confusion than ever, and I wanted to bring some clarity to the situation and simplify the process for people who are looking to get the most from their retirement.

It is my belief than an unfortunate combination of economic, demographic, and geo-political circumstances is creating the most challenging time to retire in a generation. The result could mean lower government benefits, higher taxes, fewer pensions, and increased market volatility for years to come. I can't think of a time in my twenty-five-plus years of helping people retire when the dream of a long and comfortable retirement was harder to achieve.

Baby boomers experienced unprecedented peace and prosperity in the '80s and '90s as the stock market boomed and the future looked bright. During this time of great gains in the stock market, defined benefit pension plans (which guaranteed retirees a lifetime income annuity) were slowly replaced by 401(k) plans, which were mostly invested in stock and bond mutual funds. No one seemed to mind too much back then that pensions were going away, because everyone was making so much money in the stock market. Investors just wanted to be able to continue to invest and enjoy double-digit returns in their 401(k)s.

Then came September 11, 2001—a time when the economy was already on shaky ground—which left us with a ten-year period that is now referred to as the "lost decade" in the stock market. In addition, retirees saw the major indexes lose up to 50 percent or more of their value on two separate occasions over that same ten-year period. I saw firsthand the suffering caused by the trillions of dollars that were lost in IRAs, 401(k)s, and other retirement assets during this "lost decade." And one of the things I learned during those tough years was that retirees who had enough consistent, steady, and reliable income were much happier and at peace than retirees relying too heavily on withdrawals from stock market-based investments. One of the problems today is that very few American workers are fortunate enough to have a traditional pension that will provide an acceptable level of consistent and reliable guaranteed lifetime income. Today, you are really on your own when it comes to figuring out how you will provide yourself and your family with an income you will never outlive.

The decisions you make regarding when and how to retire will have a significant impact on your quality of life and your sense of well-being in retirement. It has been my experience that many capable and successful people make these decisions without a full understanding of all their options and the long-term consequences of their choices.

One of the things I have found in helping people retire is that I get to witness firsthand how hundreds of these retirement stories turn out. I've seen a lot of happy retirement stories play out for families and I've seen some sad stories play out as well.

What I have done in developing the Retirement Freedom Solution is distilled all this knowledge, experience, and wisdom down to five key steps that, when followed, can act as a tax efficient blueprint and can help you to simplify your financial life and get the most out of what you've got.

Spending with confidence in retirement is one of the primary benefits families enjoy when following the five steps of the Retirement Freedom Solution. The key to making this plan work long-term is being able to spend with confidence regardless of the economy, whether we are in a bull market like the one in January 2018 that saw the Dow Jones Industrial Average close above 25,000 points for the first time in history, or a bear market like the one from 2008 to 2009 that saw the Dow Jones Industrial Average lose over 54 percent of its value from a high of 14,164 in October of 2007 to a low of 6,443 in March 2009. This example of market risk was a truly devastating event in the financial lives of millions American families preparing for and living in retirement.

Having a comprehensive written strategy that addresses the five most critical areas of your financial life is your best defense against the risks that threaten your financial security in retirement.

One of the most important lessons I have learned from families who enjoy fulfilling and successful retirements, regardless of the economy, is that having a comprehensive written strategy that addresses the five most critical areas of your financial life is your best defense against the risks that threaten your financial security in retirement. More importantly, having a comprehensive written strategy that addresses your biggest risks and opportunities is also your best offense when it comes to achieving the best retirement outcomes for you and your family.

The Retirement Freedom Solution

I am on a professional mission to help as many families as I can avoid the many risks they will face in retirement and help put them in a position to confidently enjoy retirement to the fullest. I know how hard you have worked to accumulate what you have, and I have made it my life's work to show you how to get the most out of what you've got. I have drawn on my quarter century of experience assisting hundreds of families make these critical decisions to develop a comprehensive step-by-step retirement planning system I call the Retirement Freedom Solution.

With some careful planning and some advanced strategies normally reserved for the privileged few, many hard-working families can work toward having a more secure and stress-free retirement.

My goal is to simplify your financial life and empower you to make smart decisions with your money so that you can enjoy the secure and happy retirement you and your family deserve. Let's get started!

Robert A. Guy,
President, RICP

Introduction to The Retirement Freedom Solution

The purpose of the Retirement Freedom Solution is to help you make smart decisions with your money. It was developed to provide you with a comprehensive, step-by-step solution to optimize your retirement income and manage the biggest risks to your retirement security.

I got the idea for the Retirement Freedom Solution based on a speech given by President Franklin D. Roosevelt on January 6, 1941, known as the "Four Freedoms" speech where he proposed four fundamental freedoms that people "everywhere in the world" ought to enjoy: (1) freedom of speech, (2) freedom of worship, (3) freedom from want, and (4) freedom from fear.[1]

I certainly would agree that people all over the world should be able to enjoy those basic freedoms. I also believe that people should be able to enjoy certain other basic freedoms when it comes to living in retirement. I designed the Retirement Freedom Solution with the

---

1   Franklin D. Roosevelt, "The Four Freedoms," (speech, 1941 State of the Union address, Washington, DC, January 6, 1941).

> **The purpose of the Retirement Freedom Solution is to help you make smart decisions with your money. It was developed to provide you with a comprehensive, step-by-step solution to optimize your retirement income and manage the biggest risks to your retirement security.**

idea of helping as many families as possible live out their retirement years with dignity, satisfaction, and peace of mind by helping them avoid the four biggest risks to retirement security and providing them with the strategies and solutions to help them get the most out of what they've got.

As such, I designed the Retirement Freedom Solution based on what I call the Retirement Freedom Bill of Rights.

The Retirement Freedom Bill of Rights

1. FREEDOM FROM THE FEAR OF RUNNING OUT OF MONEY

There is no more important retirement decision you will make than deciding when and how you will generate a lifetime of inflation adjusted income for you and your family. A combination of earlier retirements, longer life expectancies, global instability, and the elimination of traditional pensions could result in millions of boomers running out of money before running out of time.

2. FREEDOM FROM WALL STREET SPECULATION AND FEES

Wall Street charges investors billions of dollars in commissions and fees every year to speculate with their retirement dollars. For all the risk they take and fees they charge, these Wall Street firms and mutual fund companies consistently under-perform low-cost index funds.

3. FREEDOM FROM EXCESSIVE TAXATION OF RETIREMENT PLAN DISTRIBUTIONS

The United States of America has over $20 trillion in debt as of 2018, and we are adding to this debt at a staggering rate of $2 billion per day. We have made an additional $100 trillion in promised retirement and health-care benefits to current and future retirees. Washington is already starting to propose legislation to tax a larger and larger share of your retirement plan distributions.

4. FREEDOM TO REMAIN IN YOUR OWN HOME AND AVOID MEDICAID BANKRUPTCY

According to the Alzheimer's Association, 37 percent of people in the United States aged eighty-five and older are afflicted with the disease; typical life expectancy after diagnosis is four to eight years, and one in three seniors dies with some form of dementia.[2] It should come as no surprise, then, that more than one-third of your lifetime expenditures will accrue in your last few years of life.[3] One of the best ways to ensure you will be able to stay in your own home for as long as possible—and potentially avoid Medicaid bankruptcy—is to have a plan in place to deal with uninsured long-term medical expenses.

5. FREEDOM TO CREATE A LOVING LEGACY AND BE REMEMBERED FOR GENERATIONS TO COME

It should not come as a surprise that, for many of us, one or more of our children and/or grandchildren will need some financial assistance sometime in the future. It is my contention in these increasingly uncertain times that for many children and grandchildren of boomers, their parents and grandparents could be the difference between a comfortable life and a life filled with tremendous difficulty.

---

2   "2018 Alzheimer's Disease Facts and Figures," Alzheimer's Association, 2018, https://alz.org/media/HomeOffice/Facts%20and%20Figures/facts-and-figures.pdf.

3   Berhanu Alemayehu and Kenneth E Warner, "The Lifetime Distribution of Health Care Costs," *Health Services Research* 39, no. 3, June 2004, doi: 10.1111/j.1475-6773.2004.00248.x].

The Retirement Freedom Solution

The logic behind my plan is rooted in math and Nobel Prize-winning research from economists like Eugene Fama, Harry Markowitz, Merton Miller, and William Sharpe—not opinions.

THERE ARE FIVE PARTS TO THE RETIREMENT FREEDOM SOLUTION:

1. The Retirement Freedom Income Plan

2. The Retirement Freedom Investment Plan

3. The Retirement Freedom Tax Plan

4. The Retirement Freedom Long-Term Care Plan

5. The Retirement Freedom Estate & Legacy Optimization Plan

These are difficult times to be retiring. The uncertainty of what will happen to our economy, our security, and our way of life is more in question now than at any other time I can remember. When you think about the major risks of people retiring today, the number one risk is longer life expectancies. Additional years spent in retirement is increasing. At the same time, guaranteed lifetime income pensions have essentially been eliminated and replaced by 401(k) and 403(b) plans, thus shifting risk from the corporation to the employee.

Today, it is the responsibility of the employee—not the employer—to make sure they save enough money in their retirement plan every year, get good long-term investment returns, and withdraw an amount from savings that will optimize income while at the same time ensuring that you preserve enough principal to last the lifetime of you and your spouse.

Today's retirees face a complex and difficult exercise in balancing assets and cash flow over a retirement period that could last thirty or more years. Add to this the fact that the United States is already faced with a $20 trillion federal debt at a time when nearly eighty million boomers will be retiring and requiring Social Security, Medicare, and other government benefits. The federal debt is projected to explode in the coming years as baby boomers age and, subsequently, require benefits and services for longer and longer periods of time.

Today's retirees face a complex and difficult exercise in balancing assets and cash flow over a retirement period that could last thirty or more years.

All of these possibilities—people living longer, deflation, inflation, fewer pensions, more 401(k) and 403(B) plans, higher taxes, non-covered health-care expenses, and skyrocketing federal debt—are converging to create a perfect storm for retirees. Having a comprehensive written financial and estate plan is your best defense to managing the unknown. The solution to minimizing these risks is the five steps, or plans, of the Retirement Freedom Solution. Taken together, these five plans form the Retirement Freedom Solution: a program that is designed to show you how you can generate increased cash flow, cut taxes, and preserve and ultimately distribute your wealth to your heirs.

Step One: Be Free of the Fear of Running Out of Money by Creating Your *Retirement Freedom Income Plan.*

This plan looks to maximize your sources of guaranteed lifetime income. We want to identify the gap between your guaranteed lifetime income sources and your required living expenses. Then we want to look at potential ways to fill that gap through the maximization of Social Security income benefits and pension plan distributions options. If there is still a gap remaining, we want to make a decision as to whether or not to allocate some of your retirement savings toward additional sources of guaranteed lifetime income. It has been my experience that people end up with more security and peace of mind in retirement when they know they have at least their required living expenses covered for the rest of their lives.

Step Two: Be Free from Wall Street Speculations by Optimizing Your Investment Portfolio Through Your *Retirement Freedom Investment Plan.*

This plan employs evidence-based investing. Evidence-based investing refers to investing by taking note of research academia in the investment world, heeding the advice of Nobel Prize winners in the finance world, and implementing their findings on how to minimize risk and increase returns while investing. Evidence-based investing is diametrically opposed to following the strategies and methods of many Wall Street firms, big banks, brokerage firms, and most mutual fund companies. Their strategies rely on the ability to predict the future, which of course nobody can consistently do.

We don't want to allow Wall Street's conventional stock picking strategies to be your primary strategy when it comes to investing in the market. We want to use Nobel Prize-winning research that will help you reduce fees, reduce risk, and improve returns. This evidence-based investing strategy is the second important component of the overall plan.

Step Three: Be Free to Keep More of What You Earned Through Your *Retirement Freedom Tax Plan.*

With this plan, we want to turn taxable money into tax-free money and learn how to reduce taxes on required minimum distributions (RMD) and other pension plan distributions. We want to implement sophisticated tax reduction strategies to help you combat potentially rising future tax rates in a way that puts more money in your pocket. If you believe, as I do, that eventually taxes will have to go up substantially to pay our rapidly growing debt, then you will want to pay careful attention to this very important section.

Certain savings structures can put your money at risk of being taxed much more. Most people have their money in tax-deferred 401(k)s and IRAs. Those will all be taxed at some point in the future when you take the money out. The good news is you can do things now to help lower your tax bill later. With careful planning it is possible to put tens of thousands of extra dollars in your family's pocket instead of in the tax collector's pocket. The choice is yours, but you need to know what is available and how to implement these strategies in your unique situation.

Step Four: Be Free from Nursing Homes and Medicaid Bankruptcy via Your *Retirement Freedom Long-Term Care Plan.*

What we are talking about here is long-term health-care. We want to protect your retirement savings, your family, and your lifestyle and avoid Medicaid seizure of your assets. Early long-term health-care planning can also take the burden of tough decisions off your loved ones.

The goal of a long-term health-care plan is to protect your retirement savings so that they do not get eaten up by a long-term illness that is not covered by Medicare. Many people are not aware that Medicare does not cover most long-term care expenses and that it is Medicaid that pays these expenses once you are destitute. Proper planning is designed to help protect you and your loved ones from losing everything to a devastating process called "Medicaid spenddown." In addition, a good long-term health-care plan is your best chance at receiving care in your own home as opposed to a nursing home.

Step Five: Be Free to Protect Your Family and Be Remembered with the *Retirement Freedom Estate and Legacy Optimization Plan.*

What better way to be remembered than to leave a legacy that will have you loved, respected, and remembered for generations to come? With proper planning, you can turn a modest amount of money into a substantial inheritance with the intention of protecting your children and grandchildren from a very uncertain and unpredictable future. With proper planning and including a family "love letter" outlining your desires, you can make a difficult time easier for your family.

With some careful planning and advanced strategies normally reserved for the informed few, you can work toward having a more secure and stress-free retirement. Not only that, but if you follow the strategies presented in this program, you can potentially put many thousands of extra dollars in your pocket to help with your retirement expenses and increase your standard of living in retirement.

My goal for my clients is to help them manage retirement risks, increase after-tax cash flow, and take the money they have left and distribute it to their children and grandchildren in the most advantageous and efficient manner possible. I want to simplify your financial life by providing you with one simple solution to all the complex tax, investment, health-care, and retirement income challenges you will be facing in the years to come. The five easy steps of the Retirement Freedom Solution have the potential to allow you to spend more confidently in retirement and focus your time and energy on the things that matter, such as family, friends, travel, hobbies, charity, and anything else you may wish to see or do in this lifetime.

Top Four Risks to Retirement Freedom

1. LONGEVITY RISK—THE RISK THAT YOU WILL OUTLIVE YOUR MONEY

The success or failure of your retirement is not about your assets; it's about your income. Now this is a paradigm shift in thinking. Your whole life you have been taught that you must grow your pot of money bigger and bigger. But in the end, it really doesn't come down to how big your pile of money is, because your assets can be lost, stolen, divorced out, sued away, swindled from you, or devastated in a market crash.

The ultimate success of your retirement comes down to the answer to these two questions: (1) Do you have a plan to make sure you never run out of money? and (2) Have you taken the key risks off the table?

There are a lot of risks in retirement. There is market risk and withdrawal rate risk. There is the risk of inflation or deflation. And there is the risk you might need long-term health-care. While all these risks exist, there is only one pertinent risk in retirement: longevity.

The ultimate success of your retirement comes down to the answer to these two questions: (1) Do you have a plan to make sure you never run out of money? and (2) Have you taken the key risks off the table?

Why? Because longevity is not just a risk, it's a risk multiplier of all the other risks. The longer you live, the more likely the market will crash, the more likely you will take out too much money, the more likely inflation will decimate your purchasing power, the more likely you will need long-term health-care.

Today, people are living longer and longer. According to the Social Security Administration, roughly one out of every four sixty-five-year-olds at the time of this writing will live beyond age ninety, and one out of ten people will live past age ninety-five.[4] Thanks to medical innovations and increased health awareness, some of you reading this right now will live beyond the age of one hundred. In fact, centenarians are the fastest-growing age group in the United States.[5]

No matter how you look at it, Americans must find ways to support themselves for a very long time in retirement. Previous generations worked for the same company for most of their adult lives. When they retired they received a pension and Social Security that would allow them to live the rest of their lives in relative comfort. They were able to enjoy retirement without the fear of running out of money or having significant reductions in lifestyle. Most people generally retired at age sixty-five and had an average life expectancy of seventy-six years. For the most part, inflation did not have time to make a significant impact on their purchasing power. Retirees had at least two sources of income (pension and Social Security) that were guaranteed for the rest of their lives. This provided retirees with a tremendous amount of security, independence, and peace of mind throughout their retirement years. Today's retirees are faced with a

---

4   "Benefits Planner | Life Expectancy," Social Security Administration, accessed 2018, https://www.ssa.gov/planners/lifeexpectancy.html.

5   The Associated Press, "Centenarians are the fastest-growing age segment: Number of 100-year-olds to hit 6 million by 2050," New York Daily News, July 21, 2009, https://www.nydailynews.com/life-style/centenarians-fastest-growing-age-segment-number-100-year-olds-hit-6-million-2050-article-1.400828.

completely different set of challenges. And so, because longevity is not just a risk, but also a risk multiplier of all the other risks, it must be managed.

2. MARKET RISK—LOSING MONEY AT EXACTLY THE WRONG TIME

Many people do not realize that as you approach retirement all the rules you thought you knew about investing go out the window. As savers and investors, we are all taught that average rates of return matter. If you can get a 3 percent return, it's better than a 1 percent return. If you can get 5 percent, it's better than 3 percent. And if you can get 8 percent, it's better than 5 percent. So, we spend our entire investing lives thinking average rates of return matter. And they do—that is, until the day you retire and start pulling money out of your portfolio. At this point, average rates of return mean very little to you anymore. We are also taught that the stock market goes up and down, but over time the market always goes up. Well, that may be true, but not nearly as relevant anymore the day you retire and start taking money out of your portfolio.

Why? Because if you are unlucky enough to retire close to a market crash and you are relying on that money to generate income, it has been mathematically proven that you run an increased risk of running out of money. It is all about managing the sequence of returns and the timing of returns and not necessarily about the average of returns once you retire. What really matters is what happens to the markets in the critical few years leading up to your retirement and the all-important few after your retirement begins.

Sequence of Return Risk in Action

Imagine a scenario where two brothers, three years apart in age, both retire when they are sixty-two years old. At their respective retirement, both brothers have exactly $1 million in assets and have the exact same investments. Each year they withdraw the exact same amount of 5 percent, or $50,000, adjusted for cost of living, and live thirty years in retirement before passing away. This story ends happily for the older brother who retired in 1962 and who died thirty years later with a large estate. But, unfortunately, it does not end as well for the younger brother who retired in 1965, and who completely ran out of money twenty-two years later at age eighty-four.

How can this have happened? Everything was identical except for the year of retirement. In this case, market performance in the early years of retirement made all the difference since the older brother experienced positive returns during his first couple of years in retirement, while the younger brother suffered losses in his portfolio in the early years of retirement.

3. TAX RISK—THE RISK OF PAYING SIGNIFICANT TAXES ON RETIREMENT DISTRIBUTIONS

It doesn't really matter how much you have in your tax-deferred retirement accounts. The only thing that matters is how much purchasing power those dollars will provide.

For example, if you have $1 million in your IRA or 401(k), that does not represent $1 million of purchasing power for you and your family. You will only be able to spend what is left after taxes. If you end up paying 50 percent in taxes when you take those dollars out of your plan, you only really have $500,000 in purchasing power from that $1 million retirement account. It's the net amount after taxes that is most important to focus on when you are planning for a secure retirement.

In 2004, the federal debt was $7.3 trillion. This rose to $10 trillion when the housing bubble burst four years later. At the time of this writing, it exceeds $20 trillion and is growing exponentially with no end in sight. When you break this down to an *amount per taxpayer*, the numbers are substantial. That number has more than doubled over the past several years, rising from $72,051 per taxpayer in 2004 to $154,161 per taxpayer in 2017. As the debt continues higher, the liability of every taxpayer is also rising.

By some estimates, if you factor in all the promises the United States has made to all of its citizens in the form of benefits and entitlements, America is facing an $100 trillion liability in the coming years. Federal unfunded liabilities are catastrophic for future taxpayers and economic growth, and, as of this writing, are estimated at near $127 trillion, which is roughly $1.1 million per taxpayer and nearly double 2012's total world output.[6]

I believe tax-deferred retirement accounts, such as IRAs and 401(k) plans, will continue to be a prime target for Washington as they look to raise revenue to pay off the trillions in existing federal debt and fund future promises of Social Security, Medicare, and Medicaid for the boomers and beyond.

For many families today, a substantial portion of their savings is tucked away in their retirement plans. What most people don't realize is that one of your most valuable assets may constitute the biggest tax bill for you and your heirs.

Americans have nearly $20 trillion in tax-deferred retirement accounts including IRAs, 401(k)s, 403(b)s, and other retirement vehicles. Remember, tax-deferred does not mean tax-free. At some point the taxes need to be paid. The government, being in desperate need to raise revenue, is looking at all those untaxed dollars in tax-deferred retirement accounts as a potential gold mine.

What is tax-deferred? It's your deal with the IRS. This deal has a day of reckoning, and that day is called the "required beginning date." The IRS has been waiting all these years to get their money from you.

---

6   US National Debt Clock.org, accessed September 2018, http://www.usdebtclock.org.

When you turn seventy-and-a-half, the IRS has decided they have waited long enough. Sometimes the required minimum distribution amounts can generate so much additional income it can put you into a higher tax bracket, potentially causing your Social Security to be taxed at higher rates and even sparking your Medicare taxes to increase.

It is your responsibility to be just as aggressive and determined to keep your money away from the IRS as they are determined to get at it. They have a plan to get your money. Do you have a specific and detailed plan to protect it?

If you did a good job of saving, and you still have a sizable amount in your IRA at your time of death, those dollars could be subject to significant taxes. It is your responsibility to be just as aggressive and determined to keep your money away from the IRS as they are determined to get at it. They have a plan to get your money. Do you have a specific and detailed plan to protect it?

4. HEALTH-CARE RISK—THE RISK OF LOSING EVERYTHING DUE TO UNINSURED MEDICAL EXPENSES

I have learned that if you have just one missing piece to this retirement planning puzzle the whole strategy can fall apart. Perhaps the most neglected area of the retirement plan is planning for long-term health-care expenses. You can have a great income plan, investment plan, tax plan, and estate plan, but if you do not have a strategy to deal with the devastating costs associated with long-term health-care, the whole goal of financial independence for you and your family is at risk. It's a shame when I see a family that did everything else right with their financial plan lose everything at the end of the day because they just didn't realize that long-term care expenses could wipe out their savings in their last few years of life.

Despite the rapidly increasing need for long-term care services, and the rising costs of those services, most seniors and their families are still shocked to learn that Medicare doesn't pay for nursing homes or assisted living costs. Too many people mistakenly believe that Medicare will pay their medical expenses if they need long-term health-care. This misconception is costing retirees millions of dollars and forcing families all across America into bankruptcy caused by uninsured medical expenses. This truly is a national crisis that is being played out in the homes of retirees and their families all across America. The reality is that Medicare does not and cannot pay for most long-term care expenses.

Why are some people bearing enormous health-care costs while others have all of their bills paid by Medicare? Because Medicare doesn't cover what is called "custodial care" if that is the only kind of care you need. Custodial care essentially includes assistance with the toilet, eating, bathing, dressing, grooming, and moving from the chair or bed. It may also include assistance with oxygen, medications, insulin shots, and catheters.

When seniors are at their most vulnerable, and need the most care, our health-care system is not there for them. The Medicare program was designed to be there for all seniors regardless of their health-care needs. Instead, it has shrunk to exclude those afflicted with the most devastating illnesses—even though they paid into the Medicare system their whole lives.

Twelve Critical Questions

Before we move into the bulk of our discussion, take some time to review these twelve critical questions to consider as you read and begin thinking about your own retirement.

1. Will I have enough cash flow to live comfortably for life?

2. At what age should I begin taking Social Security?

3. Which pension distribution option should I choose?

4. What percentage of my required retirement income is guaranteed?

5. What is a safe withdrawal rate from my investment accounts?

6. Which accounts should I withdraw from first and why?

7. What level of risk is appropriate at this stage of my financial life?

8. Should I consider rolling over my 401(k) and/or pension to an IRA?

9. Is it a good idea to convert some of my IRAs to a Roth IRA?

10. What is my plan to stay home and avoid Medicaid bankruptcy?

11. What type of estate and legacy plan will I craft for my family?

12. Do I know how to get the most out of what I've got?

CHAPTER 1

Freedom from the Fear of Running Out of Money

THE RETIREMENT FREEDOM INCOME PLAN

When our parents and grandparents retired, many of them could rely on a pension in addition to Social Security to provide them with the bulk of their income needs in retirement. Today, many retiring baby boomers and their families may not be so fortunate. They will likely not be able to rely on a pension to supply consistent, reliable income that is guaranteed to last them for the rest of their lives. Instead, they may have to piece together a retirement income from a variety of sources, including their Social Security income benefits, withdrawals from their IRAs and 401(k)s, and withdrawals from other savings and investment accounts they may have.

Given that scenario, baby boomers need to make critical decisions regarding which accounts to withdraw from first, how much to withdraw annually, how their taxes can be minimized, and how to ensure that they will have a steady reliable income for the rest of their lives. In order to do this, we must first understand the problem we are trying to solve, being: How do you replace your salary with a stable source of income to fund your desired standard of living in retirement? That's the goal of the Retirement Freedom Income Plan—to allow you to live your optimum lifestyle, based on your goals and circumstances, for the rest of your and your spouse's lifetime. Retirement is not about your assets; it is about your income. The first thing you need to ask yourself if, "Will I have a retirement income gap?"

> **Baby boomers need to make critical decisions regarding which accounts to withdraw from first, how much to withdraw annually, how their taxes can be minimized, and how to ensure that they will have a steady reliable income for the rest of their lives.**

As baby boomers reach retirement age, many of them are facing a retirement income gap. This gap is the difference between your guaranteed lifetime income and your retirement expenses. In other words, the retirement income gap is the difference between the income you will need to fulfill your retirement dreams and the amount of income you can count on that is guaranteed.

As fewer and fewer American workers are eligible for a defined benefit pension plan that would provide them with a guaranteed income for life, most will have to retire on Social Security income plus any income they can generate from their savings and investments. Those who have savings and investments such as IRAs, 401(k)s, and other types of retirement savings will have to decide how to invest those accounts with the goal of protecting the principal and generating cash flow.

Let's take a look at the example of John and Mary Retiree and how they determined their retirement income gap. John and Mary are each sixty-six years old and have made the decision to retire from full-time work. They are looking forward to traveling, pursuing hobbies, and spending more time with their grandchildren. What will it take financially for John and Mary to be able to fulfill their retirement dreams? First, we need to take into account the fact that many retirees experience three distinct phases of retirement:

1. The go-go years—the early years of retirement when expenses will likely be highest as you do all the things you have been waiting to do.

2. The slow-go years—the middle years of retirement when you are spending more time at home and spending less money traveling and eating out.

3. The golden years—the later years of retirement when you are not spending as much on discretionary expenses, but rather primarily spending on basic living expenses and health-care costs.

Let's say we determine that John and Mary will need approximately $90,000 per year—or $5,000 per month—to pay their basic living expenses, and another $2,500 per month to fund travel, entertainment, and other discretionary expenses. Since neither John nor Mary has a traditional pension plan at work, their only source of guaranteed lifetime income is Social Security.

Let's say John is entitled to receive $2,200 per month from Social Security at the full retirement age of sixty-six, and Mary is entitled to receive $800. Since Mary's own benefit is less than half of John's benefit, Mary decides she will collect under the "spousal benefit" and receive half of John's benefit, which will be $1,100.

John and Mary Retiree's Monthly Retirement Income Gap

Their monthly income required in retirement ($5,000 + $2,500):	$7,500
Their monthly Social Security income ($2,200 + $1,100):	– $3,300
Their monthly retirement income gap:	**$4,200**

We see that John and Mary have a monthly retirement income gap of $4,200 per month. Somehow, they will have to come up with that $4,200 per month (adjusted for inflation going forward) from their personal savings and investments. Their yearly gap equals $50,400 ($4,200 X 12) and will continue to rise with inflation over time. The real challenge is that they may have to generate that rising level of income for perhaps thirty years of retirement.

John and Mary Retiree's Lifetime Retirement Income Gap

Total lifetime income required ($90,000 at 2% inflation X 30 yrs.):	$3,651,127
Total guaranteed lifetime income (Social Security at 2% X 30 yrs.):	– $1,066,496
Total amount required from savings and investments:	**$2,584,631**

The critical question: How will John and Mary generate the $2,584,631 of needed income from savings and investments? How will they fill their retirement income gap?

Some income sources are guaranteed, and some are not. Many of you are familiar with the concept of the three-legged stool of retirement income: two legs guaranteed—Social Security income and income from your company's pension plan—the third leg, usually a stock market-based account like a 401(k) or IRA, is not guaranteed income. The trouble is, most people do not have a pension anymore, making two of the three legs of the stool vulnerable to risk.

Given all the uncertainties in the world today, the first thing we want to do is maximize all our sources of guaranteed lifetime income. We don't want to run the risk of running out of money if the economy or the stock market does not work out in our favor. We want to stabilize the legs of the stool. To do so you need a retirement income plan.

The purpose of the Retirement Freedom Income Plan is to help ensure that you and your family will be able to live a comfortable and secure retirement no matter what happens with the stock and bond markets, global economy, interest rates, or taxes.

In the above example, John and Mary have only Social Security as a guaranteed lifetime income source, resulting in a $2,584,631 lifetime retirement income gap. Since their only other source of income is their retirement savings and investments, John and Mary will have to make very smart decisions with their investment and withdrawal strategies to generate the $2.5 million of inflation adjusted income they will need over the course of their retirement.

As you can see, a desired retirement income of $90,000 per year, adjusted for 2 percent inflation, will cost approximately $3,651,127 over a thirty-year retirement. If your personal retirement income goal is more than $90,000 per year, you will need to generate more than $3,651,127 of lifetime income, and if your desired retirement income is less, you will need less.

Balancing the appropriate amount of withdrawals, accounts to draw from, tax ramifications, portfolio management, and the need to make it last a lifetime is an extremely difficult and critical task.

ROBERT A. GUY, RICP®

The Retirement Freedom Solution was designed to provide you with a step-by-step system engineered to help you solve your most challenging retirement issues. Developing the appropriate income plan is the first step.

THE RETIREMENT FREEDOM INCOME PLAN CONSISTS OF THREE PARTS:

1. Social Security Maximization Strategies

2. Pension Distribution Strategies

3. Flooring Income Strategies

Let's begin reviewing these by talking about maximizing the two primary sources of guaranteed lifetime income: Social Security and pension incomes.

Social Security Maximization Strategies

Social Security has never been more important to retirement income success. With the decline of corporate pension plans, Social Security has become the foundation for most retirement income plans and, for many people, the only source of retirement income guaranteed for life and adjusted to keep pace with inflation.

What is the largest retirement asset that most Americans have? Is it their corporate pension, their 401(k), their home, or their Social Security benefit? Most think it's their 401(k) or home. The truth? Their Social Security benefit may be the largest asset that many Americans have! If you are single and have worked for thirty years, your lifetime Social Security benefit could be worth more than $500,000. If you are married, your combined lifetime benefit could exceed $1 million.

Social Security is the most reliable income stream that any of us will ever receive. Nobody can give you a guarantee as good as the government. In addition, they are promising you that cost of living adjusted check for the rest of your life. Therefore, it makes sense to try to get the maximum amount of money from Social Security as possible.

Using the appropriate Social Security claiming strategies, a couple may be able to increase their joint income benefits by as much as $100,000 or more over their lifetimes. The problem is the vast majority of retirees have no idea how to take advantage of these strategies.

Unfortunately, Congress is aware that these strategies are too good of a deal for those who take advantage of them, and at the end of 2015 they passed some very controversial changes to Social Security that are projected to cost retiring baby boomers billions of dollars in benefits every year. Section 831 of the House of Representatives' budget closed several "loopholes" in Social Security's rules about deemed filing, dual entitlement, and benefit suspension. One of the most popular Social Security maximization strategies that was eliminated is the "File and Suspend" strategy.[7]

Under File and Suspend, a claimant could file for benefits at the full retirement age of sixty-six and put off receiving them until he or she retired at age seventy. Over those years, the benefit would grow at about an 8 percent annual rate. Meanwhile, his or her spouse could claim the spousal benefit—one half of the claimant's benefit at full retirement age.

For example, let's say Mary had retired and wanted to receive her spousal benefit under John's earning record when he reached full retirement age at sixty-six. However, John was not ready to retire at sixty-six and wanted to wait until seventy to collect his benefit because each year he waited between age sixty-six and age seventy would increase his benefit by approximately 8 percent per year. Since Mary would have to wait until John filed for benefits before she could

---

7   Social Security Administration, "Bipartisan Budget Act of 2015 Closes Social Security Loophole," April 30, 2016, https://www.ssa.gov/legislation/Bipartisan%20Budget%20Act%20Closes%20Social%20Security%20Loophole%20updated.pdf.

claim her spousal benefit, John would file for benefits (allowing Mary to start collecting her spousal benefit) then he would immediately suspend his benefit and wait until age seventy to re-file and receive the higher amount.

When Congress passed the bill to eliminate File and Suspend, they said it would primarily affect the wealthy. I disagree. It is primarily going to negatively affect the middle and upper-middle class. The extra $500 to $800 per month that many families will lose because of this legislation will hit them hard. The top 1 percent probably won't miss the extra $10,000 per year, but most of the families I know will surely miss an extra $10,000.

I'm telling you this to emphasize the importance of taking advantage of whatever Social Security Maximization strategies still remain. You never know when the government will step in and take these strategies away. The good news is that people who had previously implemented these techniques were "grandfathered" and did not lose these valuable benefits.

The big question is, should you and/or your spouse claim benefits at sixty-two, full retirement age (sixty-six years old, if you are born between 1943 and 1954), or should you wait until age seventy to file for benefits?

This question deserves a thorough analysis in relation to your specific situation to determine the best course of action for you. Hundreds of thousands of dollars could be at stake over the course of your retirement. The choice of when to claim Social Security benefits is among the most important financial decisions that retirees make, yet many don't seem to give it enough thought. The talk around the coffee shop and among well-meaning friends is to take your benefits as early as you can. For a retiree who has immediate financial needs or a short life expectancy, it may be best to file for benefits as soon as possible. But for many others, current research suggests that waiting to claim Social Security can substantially increase your expected lifetime benefits and reduce the risk of outliving your money.

SOCIAL SECURITY MAXIMIZATION STRATEGY 1: DELAY, DELAY, DELAY

It's this simple: the longer you wait to claim your Social Security benefits, the higher your monthly benefit will be. As an example, by waiting to claim at age seventy instead of at age sixty-two, you can increase your lifetime monthly benefits by as much as 76 percent. Those who qualify to receive Social Security can, once they retire, start collecting benefits at any age from sixty-two to seventy. The longer someone waits to claim Social Security, the higher the monthly benefits. Someone claiming Social Security at the full retirement age (FRA), currently between sixty-six and sixty-seven, receives a full benefit, known as the primary insurance amount (PIA). The PIA is based on a retiree's earnings history and therefore varies from person to person. Someone claiming Social Security at age sixty-two receives 75 percent of their PIA while someone claiming at age seventy receives 132 percent of their PIA. For example, someone whose PIA is $24,000 per year would receive annual benefits of $18,000 by claiming at age sixty-two, $24,000 by claiming at sixty-six, or nearly $32,000 by claiming at age seventy. Claiming benefits at age seventy, as opposed to sixty-two, raises one's monthly benefit by 76 percent. That extra benefit would go on indefinitely, as long as the recipient lives. If this worker has a surviving spouse who did not qualify for the maximum benefit, the extra annual benefit would be paid for the rest of her or his life as well.

Rule of thumb: If an individual passes away well before age eighty, they will maximize lifetime benefits by starting benefits at age sixty-two. If they live past eighty, they will maximize lifetime benefits by starting benefits at seventy. If a retiring couple is married, they should make this decision together, because the age at which they apply for retirement benefits may affect the amount their surviving spouse will receive. The general rule is that the higher-earning spouse should delay applying for retirement benefits, because that is the benefit that will prevail after either spouse dies. For example, if a wife is the higher earning spouse, the longer she waits to apply—up to age seventy—the higher the retirement benefit will be for herself while she is alive and for her spouse after her death.

SOCIAL SECURITY MAXIMIZATION STRATEGY 2: OPTIMIZE SPOUSAL BENEFITS

For simplicity, I will write as if advising a wife filing on her husband's earning record, but the same rules would apply for either spouse.

First, it's important to know what a spousal benefit is. It is a payment that was originally designed for women who left the workforce to raise children or care for elderly parents. In order to receive full benefits on your own earning record you need ten years of work (forty quarters). If you worked less, or not at all, your earnings may have been very low, and your benefit would be very low or non-existent. So, Congress came up with spousal benefits to allow a recipient to receive income benefits based on their spouse's earnings record.

The amount of the spousal benefit depends on your age when you claim it. If you wait until your full retirement age (somewhere between sixty-six and sixty-seven) you will get half of what your husband could get at his own full retirement age. If you claim earlier, you'll receive less.

Where it gets tricky is if you worked ten-plus years and earned a Social Security retirement benefit of your own. Now it is not so clear whether you should claim on your own benefit or on a spousal benefit. If your husband has not retired, you can file for a benefit based on your personal earnings. When he finally does retire and goes on Social Security, the spousal amount you can receive depends on your personal benefit's size. If it's higher than what you'd get as a spouse, you'll continue to receive that same, higher amount. If your personal benefit is smaller, it will be topped up to the spousal level. If you file when your husband has already retired, Social Security will assume that you're claiming your personal and your potential spousal benefit at the same time. You will receive the higher of the two.

There is an exception for people who were born on or before January 1, 1954. It's called the Restricted Application after the Bipartisan Budget Act of 2015. If you put off your claim until full retirement age, you can file a "restricted application" for a benefit based on your spouse's earnings, without also claiming the personal benefit you're owed. At age seventy, you can switch to your personal benefit, which will have grown at approximately 8 percent per year plus the inflation rate.

What if you're divorced? If your marriage lasted at least ten years and you are now single, you get the same benefits as a current spouse. Also, you can claim the spousal benefit even if your ex-spouse has not retired, provided that they are eligible for benefits and you have been divorced for at least two years. If you have been working however, you will probably find that you will receive a higher benefit from your own earnings record.

As you can see, when and how you claim Social Security benefits is one of the most important retirement planning decisions you will make. We are talking about a 76 percent increase in guaranteed lifetime income that is being offered risk-free by the Unites States government. Why doesn't everyone do this? Because it is only those who are informed, educated, and pro-active in protecting themselves and their families that take the time to educate themselves about all the options available.

Do not permanently reduce your family's lifetime benefits by selecting the default option chosen by the masses. According to the National Bureau of Economic Research, 72 percent of eligible Americans elect to receive early benefits. This mistake costs retirees hundreds of millions of dollars a year and can be easily prevented with education and proper planning.[8]

SOCIAL SECURITY MAXIMIZATION STRATEGY 3: THE DO-OVER

Another maximization strategy is in the form of a "do-over rule." This rule allows a person sixty-two years old or older to withdraw their application for Social Security benefits and pay these benefits back as long as it's within a year of the first check. Prior to December 2010, the repayment could occur at any time, so this essentially acted as an interest-free loan. Because of the twelve-month cut-off for repayment now instated, it may still act as an interest-free loan, albeit much smaller.

This strategy is viable for someone who, perhaps, has just learned about accruing their monthly benefits as they age from year-to-year, who is past the age of sixty-two, and who would want to collect in their later years. Another example is an individual who may start receiving benefits, but then realize they want to continue working—sometimes, after thirty or more years in the workforce, they don't find a fulfilling life outside of it. This is when they would withdraw their application for their Social Security benefits and pay back what they had received thus far.

In the case that you couldn't use the do-over prior to the twelve months of application withdrawal, and you reach the full retirement

---

8   Gopi Shah Goda, Shanthi Ramnath, John B. Shoven, and Sita Nataraj Slavov, "The Financial Feasibility of Delaying Social Security: Evidence from Administrative Tax Data," NBER Working Paper No. 21544, September 2015, http://www.nber.org/papers/w21544.

age of sixty-six, you can suspend your benefits until the age of seventy. This allows you to gain the annual increase in benefits from sixty-six to seventy like you would've gotten had you waited the initial years before you started collecting.

Pension Distribution Strategies

If you have a traditional pension plan and/or a 401(k) or other tax-deferred retirement plan, some very important decisions need to be made regarding the best way to take the distribution being offered by your employer at retirement. If you are retiring from a company that has a traditional pension plan, you will be asked to decide how you want to receive your funds. You may be faced with many options including a life-only annuity, a joint-life annuity, a period-certain annuity, and a lump-sum distribution. If you have a 401(k), 403(b), or other tax-deferred retirement account, you will need to decide whether to leave the money in the old plan or rollover the money to an IRA or other retirement plan. The answers to these questions are some of the most important financial decisions you will ever make. The consequences of your decision may be long lasting and irrevocable for you, your spouse, and your family.

It is important you understand the difference between the two main types of retirement plans. A *defined benefit plan* is considered a traditional pension plan. Under this type of plan, the company provides a stated retirement benefit, usually measured in the form of a monthly payment. The final benefit amount is usually determined by a formula that can include years of service and final average salary for the last three years as the most important variables.

Under a defined benefit plan, the company sets aside money each year to fund your future promised benefits. Importantly, the risk of poor investment performance is borne by the company, not the employee. The company must pay a premium to the Pension Benefit Guaranty Corporation, a quasi-governmental organization that insures a minimum benefit level to beneficiaries of the pension plan, should something happen to the company.

Unfortunately, many workers today do not have this type of guaranteed defined benefit pension plan available. According to the Employee Benefit Research Institute, only 13 percent of private sector workers have access to a Defined Benefit Pension Plan.[9] Today, employees are far more likely to be offered a 401(k) or 403(b) from their employer. These types of tax-deferred retirement plans are considered *defined contribution plans.* Unlike defined benefit plans, where the employer takes all the risk, with defined contribution plans the employee takes all the risk. The employee is the one who is responsible for putting enough money away each year to fund a lifetime of retirement. In addition, the employee is responsible for successfully investing the funds without making any major mistakes. With defined contribution plans, the employee takes all the risk of investing, is responsible for putting enough money away each year, and must determine how to turn these funds into a safe, reliable lifetime income stream that will allow them and their spouse to enjoy a long and comfortable retirement.

Upon retirement, employees who are entitled to a traditional defined benefit pension plan, defined contribution plan, or perhaps both, will have to decide among several different distribution options. The critical question becomes: "What distribution option should I choose?"

How to best take your retirement plan distribution is one of the most complicated financial questions most people will ever face. I strongly recommend talking to a professional before making

---

9   "FAQs About Benefits—Retirement Issues: US Department of Labor Form 5500 Summaries through 1998," Employee Benefit Research Institute, accessed 2018, https://www.ebri.org/publications/benfaq/index.cfm?fa=retfaqt14fig1.

any decisions regarding retirement plan distributions. Everybody's situation is a little different and your choices should really be tailored to your unique circumstances and goals.

While a detailed discussion regarding the pros and cons of each possible distribution option is beyond the scope of this book (hundreds of books and thousands of pages of IRS code are dedicated to this one topic alone), I have provided you with a list of the basic options that may be presented to you by your employer. These are the options that are available with most retirement plans. Use this list as a starting point to educate yourself about the critically important decisions you will be facing and make sure to talk to a qualified tax advisor before making any decisions.

Depending on the specifics of any given retirement plan, the basic options are as follows:

1. Transfer the money into a separate IRA.

2. Leave the money in your current plan.

3. Annuitize the balance into a lifetime income.

4. Use some combination of options one, two, and three.

5. Take a lump-sum distribution.

6. Transfer the money to a one-person 401(k) plan.

The one-person 401(k) is an advanced strategy that is worth exploring if you have self-employment income. I have many clients who are compensated as consultants after they officially retire and can take advantage of this unique option. Many others have small businesses or other forms of employment that result in self-employment income. If you have, or will have, self-employment income after retirement, you owe it to yourself to explore the potential benefits of this option for you.

Again, due to the complexity of this issue, it is important that you speak with a qualified professional before making any decisions regarding distributions from your retirement plan. The critical point I want to make here is that you must consider your options in relation to all your other assets and sources of income, as well as your unique needs and goals for retirement.

Flooring Strategy

The happiest retirees I meet are the ones who have the most guaranteed lifetime income. But what if the combination of Social Security income and pension income (if you have any) is not enough to cover your basic living expenses? At this point you are going to have to make one of the most important financial decisions of your life. Will you utilize a portion of your retirement savings to purchase enough guaranteed lifetime income to cover at least your basic living expenses for the rest of your and your spouse's lifetimes? In other words, will you implement the flooring strategy?

The flooring strategy advises covering at least your basic living expenses with sources of guaranteed lifetime income. One way to accomplish this is to choose one of the lifetime income options being offered by your employer's defined benefit pension plan. You may also be able to re-allocate a portion of your funds in 401(k) and 403(b) accounts to generate a lifetime income stream.

The goal of the flooring strategy is to ensure that you and your spouse will always be able to maintain a certain standard of living—regardless of the economy or the stock market. This strategy gained in popularity after the stock market crash of 2008 when trillions of dollars in 401(k)s, IRAs, and other retirement assets were lost during the financial crisis.

Before we get into the details of how the flooring strategy works, let me talk about who might benefit most from this type of approach, and for whom the tactic may be more optional. First, here's an example of a couple for whom the flooring strategy may not be as critical.

Bill and Linda are getting ready to retire and are exploring their options regarding retirement income strategies. Bill worked for a well-known engineering firm for over thirty years and accumulated a good retirement package, including $4,500 per month in pension benefits with a two-thirds survivor benefit, $1.1 million in a 401(k) plan, and $180,000 in a deferred compensation plan.

Linda went back to work after their kids were in high school and put in twenty years at a local medical office. Linda had the following retirement package: $1,500 per month pension with 50 percent survivor benefit and $220,000 in a deferred compensation plan.

Bill was also entitled to $2,250 per month in Social Security benefits. Linda was entitled to $950 per month from Social Security on her own earnings record, so she elected to receive a spousal benefit of $1,125 per month based on Bill's earnings record.

After careful analysis, we determined that Bill and Linda would need $7,500 per month to pay their living expenses, which included maintaining a second home in Florida, and another $2,500 per month for travel, entertainment, and gifts for the grandchildren.

Remember, the first step in the Retirement Freedom Income Plan is to perform the retirement income gap analysis. For Bill and Linda, it looks like this:

Bill and Linda Retirement Income Gap

Desired monthly income	$10,000
Guaranteed lifetime income ($4,500 + $1,500 + $2,250 + $1,125):	− $9,375
Their monthly retirement income gap:	**$625**

Bill and Linda are in a position where they will have enough guaranteed lifetime income already coming in, so they do not need to implement a flooring strategy. Their pensions and Social Security are already doing it for them. They are only $625 per month short of meeting their income needs. In addition, Bill and Linda have nearly $1.5 million in retirement savings that they will barely need to touch in their early years of retirement.

While their large retirement account balances may provide security, they may also cause Bill and Linda some serious tax headaches later when required minimum distributions begin at age seventy-and-a-half. One risk is that taxes could be significantly higher in the future when they go to withdraw their money. Advanced tax reduction strategies will be required to combat this risk.

For clients like Bill and Linda who have more than enough lifetime income, as well as other significant assets, the next sections of the book will be of particular interest where I discuss:

- the use of low-cost index funds utilizing Nobel Prize-winning investment strategies,

- advanced tax reduction strategies,

- protection from uninsured medical expenses, and

- creating a legacy for children and grandchildren.

Unlike Bill and Linda who only have a retirement income gap of $625 per month, many people retiring today have a much larger monthly retirement income gap. Sometimes, this gap is many thousands of dollars each month. Retirees without the resources of Bill and Linda are the perfect candidates for the flooring strategy. If a couple needs $7,500 per month to live, and Social Security is only going to provide them with $3,000 per month, they have a $4,500 per month retirement income gap. Meaning, they will need to withdraw

$4,500 per month from their savings and investments, which equals $54,000 per year of withdrawals from savings and investments.

If we factor in inflation over a twenty- or thirty-year retirement, where expenses could double or more, it's easy to envision one's retirement income gap continuing to grow year after year, forcing you to withdraw more and more each year from savings and investments. This increasing income gap puts tremendous pressure on a retiree to make their portfolio last as long as they do. They will need to be extremely careful regarding investment performance, fees, taxes, and withdrawal rates to help ensure they never run out of money. It is a very delicate balancing act with severe consequences if done incorrectly. In addition, one needs a contingent plan in the event the economy and markets work against them.

Where do the majority of American workers have their retirement savings invested? They are primarily invested in stock and bond mutual funds inside a 401(k), IRA, 403(b), or some other type of retirement account. Those assets are at the mercy of the markets as evidenced by the devastation to retirees' plans after the stock market crash of 2008, which saw the S&P 500 lose over 50 percent of its value from peak to trough and saw trillions of retirement assets lost. Never before has an entire generation of retirees had so few guarantees regarding retirement income, and been so dependent on the stock market working out in their favor at just the right time.

Let's look at an example of a couple for whom the flooring strategy may be appropriate. Frank and Karen are looking to generate about $75,000 per year in income. Frank is planning on retiring later this year and Karen retired a couple of years ago. Frank has about $750,000 in savings between his IRA and some old 401(k)s, and Karen has about $190,000 in an IRA rollover from a previous employer.

The couple estimates that $50,000 per year will be needed to cover their basic living expenses and the other $25,000 per year is more discretionary in nature. Unfortunately, neither Frank nor Karen has a defined benefit pension plan from work, so their only sources of guaranteed lifetime income are Social Security benefits, as presented:

Frank and Karen's Guaranteed Lifetime Income

Frank's monthly Social Security:	$2,000
Karen's monthly Social Security:	+ $1,000
Total monthly guaranteed lifetime income:	$3,000
Total yearly guaranteed lifetime income ($3,000 $\times$ 12):	**$36,000**

We already determined that Frank and Karen need $50,000 per year to cover their basic living expenses, and another $25,000 per year for discretionary expenses. So, Frank and Karen have a yearly retirement income gap of $39,000 ($75,000 desired – $36,000 Social Security income benefits).

Frank and Karen are very nervous about the fact they only have $36,000 in annual income guaranteed, when they know they need $50,000 just to pay the bills and $75,000 in annual income to really enjoy the retirement they envision. They are also a little nervous about the direction that the world seems to be going in, and they would rather be safe than sorry when it comes to the long-term financial security of their family.

Frank decided to take a portion of his $750,000 in retirement plans and purchase some additional guaranteed lifetime income. Since Frank's employer did not offer a defined benefit pension, we did a little shopping and found that for $235,000 Frank could purchase a fixed lifetime income annuity that would provide him with $14,000 per year for the remainder of both his life and Karen's life.

Now their situation looks like this:

Frank and Karen's Guaranteed Lifetime Income

Combined yearly Social Security income:	$36,000
Combined yearly lifetime income annuity:	+ $14,000
Total guaranteed lifetime income:	**$50,000**

Frank and Karen now have enough guaranteed lifetime income to cover their basic living expenses for the rest of their lives. This accomplishes several goals for Frank and Karen. First, they have taken longevity risk off the table by providing the family enough guaranteed income to ensure they will always be able to pay at least their basic living expenses. Second, the money they removed from investments to purchase the lifetime income annuity is no longer subject to market risk. And third, the additional income means they will not have to withdraw as much annually from their savings and investments, especially in those critical early years of retirement. This income cushion takes a tremendous amount of pressure off their savings and investments in terms of annual withdrawals. The portfolio can now be allowed to grow as a long-term inflation hedge and leave a potential legacy of financial security for their children and grandchildren. Even after subtracting the $235,000 from his retirement plans, Frank will still have over $500,000 left invested in his IRA, and Mary will have $190,000 in her IRA.

ANNUITIES AS A FLOORING STRATEGY

In the next chapter, we will discuss what to do with the money remaining in the IRAs when we discuss optimizing your portfolio by utilizing low-cost index funds and Nobel-Prize winning investment strategies. For many people, taking a portion of their retirement savings and purchasing some form of additional guaranteed lifetime income makes sense. Especially if you believe, as I do, that things could get pretty tough for the markets and the economy in the coming years.

I'm sure you have heard somewhere either in the financial media, from a broker, or perhaps from well-meaning friends or family members that you should never purchase an annuity. It is important to recognize that there are many different types of annuities out there. Some types of annuities you may want to avoid altogether. Others you may want to consider in the context of a well-thought-out retirement income strategy. Annuities are a unique financial instrument in that they can do things no other financial instruments can do—specifically, provide you and your loved ones with an income stream you can never outlive.

An annuity can guarantee you a paycheck for the rest of your life. There is no other financial instrument that can do that. Stocks can't do it. Bonds can't do it. Real estate can't do it. CDs can't do it and money markets can't do it. Even gold can't do it. The only financial instrument that can guarantee you and your spouse a monthly check for the rest of your life is an annuity, upon the claims-paying ability of the insurance company. So, if you don't have adequate Social Security benefits and/or pension benefits to cover your basic living expenses for both your and your spouse's lifetime, then you owe it to yourself and your family to consider this strategy as a way to protect a minimum standard of living.

Don't just take my word for it. Read what *Time*, *Barron's*, and even the Government Accountability Office have to say about securing an adequate amount of guaranteed lifetime income.

A *Time* magazine article stated, "Securing at least a base level of lifetime income should be every retiree's priority—at least if they want to live happily ever after."[10]

The June 20, 2011, issue of *Barron's* focused on annuities: "With investors clamoring for steady flows of income, it's time to give annuities a fresh look."[11]

Also in June 2011, the Government Accountability Office released its report on retirement income. Saying, in part, "Social Security is not enough [for people to retire on]." They recommended that people "work longer, save more, and delay receipt of Social Security benefits until at least the full retirement age." It went on to say that "seniors should use a portion of their savings to purchase a lifetime income annuity to cover necessary expenses."[12]

And there you have the flooring strategy: optimize retirement income, guarantee a base level of income for life, and be free to enjoy retirement to the fullest. The strategic combination of advanced Social Security, pension distribution, and flooring income strategies is the core of the Retirement Freedom Income Plan.

Once we have developed the appropriate retirement income plan for you, it is time to focus on what to do with the rest of your money. Let's get investing!

10 Dan Kadlec, "Lifetime Income Stream Key to Retirement Happiness," *Time*, July 30, 2012, http://business.time.com/2012/07/30/lifetime-income-stream-key-to-retirement-happiness/.

11 Karen Hube, "Best Annuities," *Barron's*, June 20, 2011, https://www.barrons.com/articles/SB50001424053111904472004576392401608661120.

12 "Retirement Income: Ensuring Income throughout Retirement Requires Difficult Choices," US Government Accountability Office, July 1, 2011, https://www.gao.gov/products/GAO-11-400.

CHAPTER 2

Freedom from Wall Street Speculation and Fees

THE RETIREMENT FREEDOM INVESTMENT PLAN

The goal of the Retirement Freedom Investment Plan is to invest retirees in a well-diversified portfolio of low-cost index funds to help combat the long-term effects of inflation on their purchasing power.

As we saw in chapter 1, a properly executed Retirement Freedom Income Plan that attempts to maximize Social Security income and pension income—along with a strategy to fill in any income gaps with additional sources of guaranteed lifetime income—goes a long way toward reducing retirement risks. In fact, the Retirement Freedom Income Plan can reduce or eliminate the number one risk for retirees—longevity.

However, there is another risk that retirees need to be particularly well prepared for—inflation. Inflation is one of the biggest risks many retirees will face, and the one risk that I find people underestimate. Due to inflation, many baby boomers could see their cost of living double or even triple over their lifetimes. The Retirement Freedom Investment Plan is designed to help retirees deal with the risk of inflation, as well as reduce market risk and investment fees associated with your portfolio.

I want to structure your investment portfolio to grow at a pace that will help you outpace inflation. More importantly, I want to change the way you think about investing. I believe the traditional financial services industry is failing to serve retirees properly. In this chapter, I will show you what I believe is another way to invest with confidence.

I have noticed that many of the people who come in to see me are making the same mistakes. They are taking unnecessary risks: not diversifying their portfolios properly, buying and selling at the wrong time, and paying too much in fees and taxes—resulting in poor investment results with too little return and too much risk.

DALBAR, Inc., is the financial community's leading independent expert for evaluating and auditing mutual fund investors performance results. Since 1994, DALBAR's annual Quantitative Analysis of Investor Behavior (QAIB) report has measured the effects of investor decisions to buy, sell, and switch into and out of mutual funds over short- and long-term timeframes. QAIB 2016 examined real investor returns in equity, fixed income, and asset allocation funds. The analysis covered the thirty-year period to December 31, 2015, encompassing the crash of 1987, the drop at the turn of the millennium, the crash of 2008, plus recovery periods of 2009, 2010, and 2012. The results consistently show that the average investor earns less—in many cases, much less—than the performance of the underlying mutual funds. It concluded: "Investment results are more dependent on investor behavior than on fund performance. Mutual fund investors who hold on to their investments have been more successful than those who try to time the market."[13]

Why does the average investor under-perform the "market" so dramatically? I hold the financial media and Wall Street to blame for much of this problem. The truth is that the majority of financial and investment advice is generated to produce the illusion that experts and investment firms have a forecast or a prediction. Television financial news programs are pushing their information on television akin to a carnival barker pushing a freak show. The reality is that whether it is an analyst, a brokerage firm, a CEO, or a mutual fund manager, no one has any true insight as to which stocks will perform well in the future or where the markets are going next. These forecasts or predictions are statistically worthless. Even worse, they could cost you your life's savings.

No one can consistently give you an accurate forecast of the market or of any individual stocks. While all these parties imply that their methods of stock picking, market timing, research, and analysis could provide you with a significant advantage that you can employ to make money, the reality is often buried within their own marketing materials. If you read the prospectus, it will say, "past performance is no indicator of future results." That certainly is true.

Whether it is *Money* magazine, CNBC, or any other type of financial media, they have an agenda—to get you to watch their program or buy their magazine. They are in the business of selling advertising. And as a result, they have turned the financial advice business into another form of entertainment.

Wall Street is totally onboard with this media strategy because

13   "2016 QAIB Report Advisor Edition 4685," DALBAR, Inc., 2016, http://www.northstarfi-nancial.com/files/6314/6523/9571/2016_DALBAR_Advisor_Edition.pdf.

when you act on their advice and purchase something the media recommends, Wall Street will be there to handle the transaction and, in the process, take their fair share of the cut. In addition, the brokerage firms and mutual fund companies that make up Wall Street spend billions annually on advertisements in these publications.

The Wall Street model is designed to line the pockets of the big firms with cash rather than to help you enjoy a comfortable and secure retirement. Most Wall Street firms and mutual fund companies are big believers in something called "active" management. Active managers attempt to "beat the market" through a variety of techniques such as stock picking and market timing.

Active investing means that someone constantly monitors handpicked investments, ready to initiate different strategies based on different market conditions, with the goal of outperforming the market, usually in the short-term.

At first glance, the definition of active investing or active management might sound appealing—lots of customized attention; lots of monitoring; a tailored, intensive strategy; and all of the positive associations that come with the root word, *action*. But let's step back: What are the real-world circumstances of active investing?

When you treat investing like a game, someone will lose. Nobody can outsmart the market. The house always wins.

The biggest red flag is the idea of a portfolio manager picking a few stocks and breaking a sweat every day trying to anticipate which move to make next. Even if this person is a genius, there is too much risk and too much room for human error. In this scenario, investing becomes more like a game than a retirement investment plan—and every game has losers. When you treat investing like a game, someone will lose. Nobody can outsmart the market. The house always wins.

I believe most investors would be better off adopting a different investment philosophy called "evidence-based investing." The evidence-based model avoids subjective forecasts, takes a longer-term view, and works to deliver market-like returns.

Evidence-based investing is also known as passive investing, which is a style of management associated with mutual and exchange-traded funds (ETF) where a fund's portfolio mirrors various market indexes. Passive management is the opposite of active management, in which a fund's manager attempts to beat the market with various investing strategies and buying/selling decisions of a portfolio's securities.

Evidence-based (passive) investing means creating a diverse portfolio modeled on index funds that is built for long-term performance and does not require much tweaking. The core idea is that a diverse portfolio, built with a long-term perspective in mind, is a comfortable way to invest. This concept is based on index funds, which are designed to historically match the performance of the market. The portfolio is tailored to the customer's risk tolerance and need for both growth and income. And there is a savings because it does not call for the extra expense of active manager fees. Fees in index funds are generally much lower than the fees in actively managed funds, thereby potentially saving you tens of thousands of dollars over the course of your retirement. The manager sets it up right the first time and lets the market take its course.

The Efficient Market Hypothesis, as put forth by Nobel Prize-winning economist Eugene Fama of the University of Chicago Booth School of Business, asserts that no investor will consistently beat the market over long periods except by chance. Active managers go against this hypothesis every day through their efforts to outperform their benchmarks and deliver superior risk-adjusted returns. Data compiled by Morningstar showed less than 25 percent of the top-performing active managers are able to consistently outperform their passive manager counterparts.[14]

In my opinion, investors would do well to be rid of the belief that you can beat the market or that some analyst has a strategy to help your broker or mutual fund company predict which investments are going to do better over time. There is no one who can consistently get you in the market when things are about to go up or get you out of the market when things are about to go down—that expectation is unrealistic. It just simply cannot happen on a consistent basis. What can happen is you can get a broadly diversified portfolio of low-cost index funds and exchange-traded funds where your goal is to capture the returns of the market, not beat the market. Then you strategically rebalance the portfolio over time and make minor adjustments along the way to suit your needs.

Here are the six deadly misconceptions that investors tend to believe:

1. Stock-picking works.
2. Timing the market works.
3. Research works, no matter the firm you're talking to.
4. Track record investing works.
5. Forecasting works.
6. Markets don't work; they're inefficient.

All of these misconceptions can get in your way as an investor. Most brokerage firms and mutual fund companies don't want you to know the truth because they make a lot of money off those beliefs. Trillions of dollars are invested on your belief that they can time the

---

14   Ben Johnson, Michael Rawson, Thomas Boccellari, and Alex Bryan, "Morningstar's Active/Passive Barometer," Morningstar, June 2015, https://hkbeta.morningstar.com/ods_images/2015Jun_Morningstar%20Active-Passive%20Barometer.pdf.

market, pick individual stocks, and know when to get in and get out. The truth is: nobody can consistently do that.

One thing to remember about active managers is that they are constantly buying and selling stocks within those mutual funds. Not only do you pay for these commissions as part of your expense ratio, but you also incur additional expenses on what's called the *spread*—the difference between the buy and the sell price the portfolio manager had to pay on the purchase. Thus, there are a lot of hidden expenses and fees that investors are paying on these actively managed funds.

In 1990, the Nobel Prize in Economics was awarded to Harry Markowitz, Merton Miller, and William Sharpe for their role in developing the concept of modern portfolio theory. Modern portfolio theory is a long-term investment strategy that includes diversification and asset allocation. Markowitz, Miller, and Sharpe determined asset allocation was a more important predictor of success or failure in the market than picking stocks. In their Nobel Prize-winning research, stock selection was shown to have a very small impact on your success or failure as an investor. Instead it came down to how assets were allocated across different asset classes. Many investors are surprised to learn that a tremendous amount of evidence supports the efficient market hypothesis.

You can choose to listen to the so-called experts from the big banks, brokerage firms, and financial media, or you can choose to listen to the research of Nobel Prize-winning PhDs and economists from some of the most respected institutions in the world.

Asset class investing, utilizing evidence-based investment strategies, refers to a buy-and-hold approach to asset management. If you think the markets work efficiently, then buying and selling securities in an attempt to outperform the market is effectively viewed as a game of chance rather than skill. Instead of trying to forecast the future, the asset class investing approach involves applying scientific, academically proven strategies of modern portfolio theory.

When I talk about asset classes, I am talking about many different asset classes: large company stocks, medium company stocks, small company stocks, growth-based stocks, value stocks, domestic and international stocks. When it comes to bonds and fixed income, there are long-term bonds, short-term bonds, intermediate-term bonds, corporate bonds, and government bonds. You also have various sectors, whether it's real estate, technology, or health-care.

In passive management, instead of trying to beat the market, you diversify using asset allocation to capture the market's returns. You expose the portfolio to different types of investments including equities and fixed income, domestic and international, and growth and value to provide diversification and put in some non-correlated assets. The goal is to maximize returns for any given level of risk. In doing so, the first step is to determine your risk tolerance, and then build your portfolio based around your risk tolerance and need for growth.

The three tenets of asset class investing are: market returns, asset allocation, and lifelong investing. Lifelong investing is a step beyond long-term investing, as it is seen as a life-long process. Instead of attempting to get in and out of the market at the right time, most people should be staying in the market in one form or another for the rest of their lives. This is in contrast to the three tenets of speculative investing, which are stock selection (picking stocks that will get you high returns in the future), track record investing (utilizing an investment's previous performance to determine whether or not to invest in it in the future), and market timing (an attempt to alter or change a portfolio based on a prediction about the future, which nobody can do).

After you have determined your risk tolerance, you want to build a broadly diversified portfolio utilizing index funds and/or exchange traded funds. Then you want to monitor your portfolio and rebalance your allocations as needed. How?

Let's say you've determined that you should have 20 percent in large cap growth, 15 percent in large cap value, 10 percent in small cap growth, and 5 percent in small cap value. You basically put a limit on how far out of your range you are comfortable getting. If you wanted to have 20 percent in something and it climbs to 25 percent for example, that's when you would rebalance. It's not a calendar thing; it's based more on how far from your target that your investments get that would trigger when you would rebalance it. At different times, different asset classes perform well. In a situation where growth stocks have performed extremely well, human nature says, *Those are doing the best, so let's leave it alone.* But what we know is that if it has done the best over the past, it is likely not to do as well over the future. No one knows exactly what will happen, but it is prudent to stick with your 20 percent allocation. If you get too far out of that range, it is time to realize some of your gains and move it so that you are back closer to your target with your desired allocation. Another example of when you might rebalance is if you have decided you do not want 25 percent large cap growth anymore but only want 15 percent. Therefore, you might change your allocations. That would be another reason to rebalance.

Let's go back to one of the key risks in retirement planning: inflation. Inflation risk is managed by having the appropriate asset allocation for your specific risk tolerance, income needs and time frame. I use assets such as stocks, bonds, index funds, real estate, and commodities to help fight long-term inflation. A properly allocated and rebalanced portfolio of low-cost index funds is designed to grow over time to help you combat the long-term effects of inflation on your purchasing power.

One of the retirement investment strategies that many investors have lost faith in is the *4 percent withdrawal strategy*. Prior to the 2008 market crash, it was common for retirees to assume that if they did not take more than 4 percent per year out of their portfolio, they would have a high likelihood of never running out of money. For example, if someone had a $1 million diversified portfolio, they could expect to be able to safely withdraw $40,000 per year with a relatively low risk of running out of money over a normal life expectancy.

However, recent studies after the market crash of 2008 suggest a 2 percent or 3 percent withdrawal rate is more prudent. This low withdrawal rate would result in only $20,000 to $30,000 of income per $1 million of investments saved. I have found what I believe to be a much better way.[15]

THE BUCKET STRATEGY

Each investment plan that I develop consists of four buckets. Each bucket is designed with investments that are intended for the time frame in which you will spend money from those portfolios.

Depending on your needs and objectives, your retirement savings will be split among these four buckets. Money that you will spend sooner in retirement will be invested more conservatively than money that you will be spending later in retirement. The money that you will spend later in retirement, because you will have ten or twenty years before you will need it, will be invested a little more aggressively.

For example, the first bucket is filled with very secure investments that are designed to provide you with a safe, steady, and predictable income for the first five years of your retirement. The investment objective for this bucket is *income with capital preservation*.

---

15   Jeff Benjamin, "Redoing the Math on a 4% Retirement Withdrawal Rate," Investment News, July 19, 2017, https://www.investmentnews.com/article/20170719/FREE/170719919/redoing-the-math-on-a-4-retirement-withdrawal-rate.

The next bucket, which will be used for income in the second five years of retirement, will be made up of different investments. Since you have the first five years to let bucket two grow, you can use an investment portfolio that is designed to grow for five years and then provide income for the second five years of your retirement. The investment objective for bucket two is *income with moderate growth*.

Buckets three and four work the same way. Any money in those portfolios will grow while you are spending money from the earlier buckets. When needed, you can then take a portion from these portfolios to provide income in five-year durations.

Since buckets three and four have anywhere from ten to twenty years or more to grow before you will need to take any income from them, these portfolios are designed to give you the greatest potential for growth over that time frame. Buckets three and four are where the real inflation hedge comes from. The investment objectives for buckets three and four are *growth with income* and *growth*, respectively.

The last step is to determine specifically how much money needs to be allocated to each of the buckets. I use a sophisticated software program that can look at your income needs and all available income resources throughout each year of your retirement. We can factor in inflation and look at various rates of return to determine specifically what your needs are. With this information, we can determine the appropriate amount of money to allocate to each bucket.

Let's go back to Frank and Karen from our previous example. They would like to generate $75,000 of income to fulfill their retirement dreams. Social Security is going to provide them with only $36,000 of that need. Thus, they have a retirement income gap of $39,000 per year.

We decided to utilize the flooring strategy and used $235,000 of Frank and Karen's $940,000 of retirement savings to purchase an additional $14,000 of guaranteed lifetime income that would last for both of their lives. By utilizing the flooring strategy, Frank and Karen now have enough guaranteed lifetime income to cover their $50,000 of basic living expenses.

However, they still need to generate an additional $25,000 per year to cover their discretionary expenses and the full $75,000 needed to pay for both fixed and discretionary income needs. This is where the bucket withdrawal strategy from a properly allocated portfolio of index funds comes in. Wanting to optimize their investments with an eye toward inflation, we can use the bucket strategy to provide them with the additional income they needed.

Let's allocate Frank and Karen's remaining $705,000 of retirement assets into four separate "buckets" of money, each to be used at different times throughout their retirement years.

They place enough money into the first bucket to cover their first five years of expenses. Since bucket one is made up of secure investments such as cash, treasuries, CDs, and short-term bonds, they will not have to worry about selling any investments to meet their income needs if or when the market drops.

Since they won't need the money from bucket two for at least five more years, they invested that money a little more for growth. The same goes for buckets three and four—they won't need the money from bucket three for at least ten years, and the money from bucket four for at least fifteen years.

With the combination of enough lifetime guaranteed income to cover their basic living expenses, and an investment strategy designed to provide them with secure predictable income to act as an inflation hedge, they are positioned to enjoy peace of mind in retirement. They will have the freedom to spend their money and enjoy their golden years to the fullest.

In conclusion, when investing for your retirement, don't try to time the market. Don't try to get in and out. And don't let your emotions take over. People tend to get very emotional about their money. The two overriding emotions in investing are fear and greed. Investors either panic and get out at the exact wrong time, or they get greedy and load up on something that they think is going to grow to the sky. Of course, it is not. Forget all that emotional stuff. And forget everything the brokerage firms, mutual fund companies, and the financial media are telling you. Listen to the academics and the Nobel Prize winners, most of whom have a belief that markets are efficient. The best way to invest is to implement the Retirement Freedom Investment Plan, and have a broad, diversified portfolio of passively managed index funds. Rebalance this on an ongoing basis and stay invested for the rest of your life. Then relax and enjoy your retirement without the fear of running out of money. Now let's reduce your taxes!

CHAPTER 3

The Freedom to Keep More of What You've Earned

THE RETIREMENT FREEDOM
TAX PLAN

In March of 2017, the Investment Company Institute reported that US retirement assets totaled $25.3 trillion as of December 31, 2016—up 1.4 percent from the end of September, and up 6.1 percent for the year. Individual Retirement Accounts (IRAs) accounted for 34 percent of all household financial assets in the United States at the end of 2016.[16]

If you consider the facts that close to eighty million baby boomers are retiring at a rate of ten thousand per day, and that people are routinely living into their eighties and nineties, federal and state gov-

---

16   "2017 Investment Company Fact Book: A Review of Trends and Activities in the Investment Company Industry," ed. 57, Investment Company Institute, https://www.ici.org/pdf/2017_factbook.pdf.

ernments are going to need to raise large sums of tax revenue to make good on their promises. Eighty million boomers, along with their children and grandchildren, have already been promised more than $100 trillion in benefits. The money is going to have to come from somewhere. The taxes stuffed inside the $25 trillion in tax-deferred retirement accounts are the perfect place for politicians to start.[17]

You may be thinking to yourself, *Hey, I thought they just passed a tax cut at the end of 2017.* That may be true, but remember: The tax reform act of 2017 has a sunset provision on the individual tax cuts. Only corporate tax cuts were made permanent. Individual tax cuts sunset and go away in 2025. If you will be taking distributions from a tax-deferred retirement plan such as an IRA or 401(k) any time after 2025, you are at risk of losing a substantial portion of those assets to taxes.

Required Minimum Distributions: The Time to Act Is Now.

If you could design a perfect tax retirement plan it would look like this: contributions that are tax deductible, accumulation that is tax deferred, and distributions that are tax free.

Unfortunately, such a plan encompassing all three of these qualities does not exist. I would argue that, for many people, it makes sense from a tax perspective to forgo the current tax deduction on contributions in favor of tax deferral on accumulations and distributions that are tax-free. The essence of my Retirement Freedom Tax Plan is to help reduce your taxes in retirement by reducing your taxable required minimum distributions.

What are required minimum distributions (RMDs)? It's the

---

17 D'vera Cohn and Paul Taylor, "Baby Boomers Approach 65 – Glumly," December 20, 2010, http://www.pewsocialtrends.org/2010/12/20/baby-boomers-approach-65-glumly/.

way you get taxed on your IRA and other retirement plan distributions. Managing your required minimum distributions is the key to advanced tax planning and managing those RMDs may save you significant taxes in retirement.

Factors every retiree should know about RMDs is that RMDs are included in the provisional income test to determine Social Security benefit taxation, and are tested for Medicare premiums.

It is not just about paying income taxes on your required distribution; your RMD can also:

- push you into a higher tax bracket,

- cause your Social Security to be taxed at a higher rate,

- cause your Medicare premiums to go up,

- increase net investment income surcharges, and

- increase alternative minimum taxes.

Historically, it made sense for most people to spend after-tax money in retirement before withdrawing IRA or 401(k) money. The logic is that your aim is to allow the tax-deferred money to grow on a tax-deferred basis as long as possible. But that's not always the case in the new financial world we are living in.

When we are talking about retirement plans and taxes, we have to study the required minimum distribution rules. Whether or not you want the money or need the money, at age seventy-and-a-half (by April 1 of the year following the year you turn seventy-and-a-half) the IRS will require you to start taking money out of your IRAs. Every year thereafter, you will be required to take your RMD by December 31. Those distributions will generate taxable income whether you need the money or not. So, it's important to understand how those

RMD rules work. Managing these RMDs is critically important for your overall tax situation.

As an example, say Mary and Bill are doing some retirement and estate planning and are concerned about their required minimum distributions and the impact they will have on their taxable income during retirement.

They are both seventy years old, and they have not been taking any money out of their IRAs yet because they haven't needed the money. They have other income. They have pension income. They have Social Security income. They have savings outside of their retirement plans, so they haven't needed to access their IRA money. Because of this, they have been able to defer paying taxes on this money until now.

The reason the government makes you start taking the money out of your tax deferred retirement plans at this age is because they want to start collecting their taxes on that money. It's been deferred all these years, but is not tax-free. The IRS now wants the money, so they force you to start taking money out and pay taxes on the distributions.

Mary and Bill are surprised to learn the RMD amount on their tax-deferred retirement plans will be approximately $27,000 in the first year alone, and the percentage that needs to come out will increase each year. This required distribution adds approximately $27,000 of taxable income to all their other taxable income, pushing them into a higher tax bracket and significantly increasing their quarterly estimated tax payments. To add insult to injury, RMD income can also cause an increase in Social Security and Medicare taxes.

Again, you are required by law to start taking required minimum distributions from your tax-deferred retirement plans by April 1 of the year following the year you turn seventy-and-a-half. If you turned seventy-and-a-half in 2016, you'd have to take your first distribution by April 1 of 2017. Then, every year thereafter, you will be required to take your annual distribution by December 31.

Bill and Mary are taking an RMD distribution in 2016 as required by law. The amount will be based partly on their December 31, 2015, balance. The way to calculate their distribution in 2016 is to take their 2015 year-end balance and divide it by the appropriate number on something called the Uniform Lifetime Table. In effect, the Uniform Table is an age-dependent projected distribution period and is based on the joint life expectancy projection of an IRA owner and a hypothetical beneficiary not more than ten years younger. At age seventy-one, the projected distribution period is twenty-six-and-a-half years. Many companies have calculators that allow you to calculate that as well. If you're working with a firm, they can calculate it for you, or you can even look up the Uniform Table on the IRS website if you want to do the calculation yourself.

RMDs generate a lot of taxable income, so one of the primary strategies of the Retirement Freedom Tax Plan is to reduce or eliminate required minimum distributions by strategically moving money over time from tax-deferred accounts to tax-free accounts.

RMD ELIMINATION STRATEGY 1: ROTH IRA CONVERSION

The first RMD elimination strategy or tax reduction idea is the Roth IRA conversion. A Roth conversion of even a portion of your traditional IRA or retirement plan may offer significant financial advantages, partly because the money that is in a Roth IRA is not subject to required minimum distributions. Any money you convert from a traditional 401(k), IRA, or 403(b) to a Roth IRA or 401(k) will no longer be subject to required minimum distributions. And any money that you do withdraw is tax-free as long as certain minimum conditions have been met.

The Roth IRA was written into law in 1998 as an incentive for

Americans to save more for retirement. I've run countless projections for clients regarding the pros and cons of Roth IRAs versus traditional IRAs and other tax-deferred retirement plans. After careful analysis, I've concluded that, for many tax payers, the Roth IRA and Roth IRA conversion offer more purchasing power for clients and their families because they create tax-deferred growth and tax-free distributions.

The rationale for doing a Roth IRA conversion is that you want to pay the tax now on the amount of money in your IRA. If you have $100,000 in an IRA, you might predict that your IRA will grow to $150,000 or $200,000 over time. The money that is growing tax-deferred in those plans is going to have to start coming out at age seventy-and-a-half unless you convert some of that money to Roth accounts. If you convert your regular IRA to a Roth IRA (or some portion of it), the money that is in the Roth IRA is not going to have to come out as a required distribution. Converting allows you to take control of your taxes. It's true you are paying taxes now on the amount you convert, but wouldn't you rather pay tax on today's lower amount at today's known tax rates? The alternative is to pay taxes on larger account balances in the future at the unknown tax rates of the future. That's the rationale for converting traditional tax-deferred accounts to Roth Accounts. If you believe tax rates will be higher in the future, as I do, then you may want to consider this strategy.

The Zero Tax Plan

With some advanced tax planning, you can convert just enough of your traditional plans to Roth IRAs so that the new, lower RMDs won't push you into a higher tax bracket. Remember, the Roth IRAs are not subject to RMD, so only the money remaining in the old plans, if any, will be subject to taxable RMDs. This works particularly well for people who do not currently need the money. Going forward you can control your taxable income, which can keep you in a lower tax bracket and reduce your income taxes for years to come.

You may be able to structure your RMD by an amount that would help you avoid paying taxes on up to 85 percent of your Social Security benefits.

Depending on your income needs, you may be able to structure your RMD by an amount that would help you avoid paying taxes on up to 85 percent of your Social Security benefits. Here's how it works: Depending on your income, you pay taxes on your Social Security income at a rate of either 50 percent or 85 percent. With proper planning, you can get your taxable income down to the point where you are only paying taxes on 50 percent of your Social Security benefit. Or perhaps, even to a level where you won't be subject to tax on Social Security benefits at all.

Some people may ask, "Why would I want to pay taxes now?" But when you do a Roth conversion, what's important is that you only pay taxes on the amount that you convert now. So, the reason you may be willing to pay income tax now is because all the growth on the account from the day of the conversion and all withdrawals by you and your heirs could be completely tax-free. The key to this tax reduction strategy is that we know what the tax rate is today; we have no idea what the tax rate will be tomorrow.

At least you have some control over what taxes you are going to pay on retirement income. If you think taxes may go up in the future to help pay the $100 trillion in unfunded government liabilities, then it may make sense to pay taxes now at known rates and have all future growth be tax-free for you and your heirs.

Pay Taxes on the Seed, Not the Harvest.

An agricultural analogy to make this point is that a Roth IRA conversion requires you to be taxed on the seed. In this case, the seed is the amount you convert to the Roth IRA. You plant the seed, which is the investment in the new Roth, and over the years it blossoms and grows. Then, when you or your heirs harvest the crop (the original investment and all the growth), the harvest is tax-free income. Of course, you always must run the numbers for your specific situation, and see the cost/benefit analysis of paying taxes now versus paying taxes later on your distributions.

With a Roth conversion, you can change all or just a portion of your IRA or other retirement plans to a Roth account, and when you make the conversion you must add the amount of money you converted to your other income and pay taxes on it. After paying the tax, you'll have converted your traditional account to a Roth IRA.

Purchasing Power versus Dollars

Purchasing power is what matters, as opposed to the total number of dollars. For me, the secret to understanding advanced tax planning is to value wealth in terms of purchasing power rather than dollars. I look at purchasing power versus money. It is not what you have; it is what you can spend after taxes that counts. The concept of understanding what your IRA and other retirement plan assets will provide you in terms of real, after-tax spendable income is critical to understanding the rationale behind advanced tax planning.

When it comes to money, we tend to think that whoever has the biggest pile wins, right? I'm going to offer a different way of analyzing the question. Maybe having the most money is not the best way to measure your affluence or wealth. Perhaps the better way to measure wealth or affluence is by assessing your total purchasing power, not your total dollars. It really does not matter

> Perhaps the better way to measure wealth or affluence is by assessing your total purchasing power, not your total dollars. It really does not matter what the dollar number is; it matters what it can buy.

what the dollar number is; it matters what it can buy. Once you reach retirement, the only thing that matters is how much after-tax net spendable income that big pile of money is going to provide you and your family for the rest of your lives.

Understanding this concept is key to understanding advanced tax strategies for retirement plans. Let's say you have $1 million in a traditional IRA. Even though you have that amount of money in dollars, in practical terms you don't have $1 million of purchasing power.

Because the money in your traditional IRA is tax-deferred, not tax-free, you will have to pay income tax when you withdraw that money. Essentially, you have a big mortgage or IOU to the IRS to the tune of hundreds of thousands of dollars. Even though you have $1 million in your tax-deferred retirement account, you actually have far less than that amount available to travel the world or help your grandkids or give to charity.

Say a couple has $200,000 in an after-tax, non-tax-deferred brokerage account. In all they have $200,000 in an after-tax account, and $300,000 in a tax-deferred plan, such as an IRA.

When measuring money the conventional way, we might say they have a total of $500,000. And while it is correct to say $500,000 represents the total number of dollars they have, perhaps a more accurate measuring tool of their wealth is their purchasing power. If they have an effective tax rate of 25 percent, they could owe as much as $75,000 in taxes when those dollars are distributed, possibly even more if tax rates go up in the future.

It would be more accurate to say they have $425,000 worth of purchasing power versus $500,000, after we consider the $75,000 tax liability to the IRS. Let's assume they want to buy something. If they withdraw the money out of their IRA, they are only going to get $225,000 after tax. Combined with the $200,000 in their after-tax account, they have $425,000 of purchasing power.

If they decide to convert the $300,000 IRA to a Roth IRA and pay the $75,000 in taxes out of the after-tax money, one could argue on the first day of the conversion they have the exact same purchasing power. They each have the same $425,000 of purchasing power, yet all future growth on the initial seed of an investment in the Roth IRA could potentially blossom into a harvest of tax-free income for them for decades to come.

Their initial reaction was to say, "I'm out $75,000?" But the concept is they are not. Their purchasing power is exactly the same as it was before the Roth conversion. They can buy $425,000 worth of goods and services. It doesn't matter that their statement says $500,000. There's a $75,000 IOU to the IRS on that money.

Don't underestimate the power and advantages of the Roth IRA conversion in the right situation. The difference could be many tens of thousands of dollars to you and your family. You must run the numbers for your specific situation and make the decision that works best for you.

RMD ELIMINATION STRATEGY 2: TAX-FREE LIFE INSURANCE FUND (TLIF)

Another effective tool to eliminate huge taxes in retirement is life insurance. I know what you are thinking: *Life insurance in retirement? Why would I want that?* Because you want to take advantage of one of the single biggest benefits in the tax code: the tax-exemption for life insurance. I'm talking about the new modern insurance policies designed to meet the needs of eighty million retiring boomers. Today's policies have living benefits that can be designed to give you access to tax-free income as well as long-term care benefits while you are living *and* a tax-free death benefit to your family when you are gone.

Many people have never considered using their IRA to build

a tax-free life insurance fund for retirement (TLIF). However, this is a tool that shares many of the same attributes as the Roth IRA. It lowers your future RMDs by paying off the tax now at today's known rates. Like distributions from Roth IRAs, distributions from life insurance can also be tax-free and are not included in the calculation to determine the taxation of Social Security and Medicare benefits. Life insurance can be an effective tool to get you as close to zero taxes in retirement as possible.

I like to compare today's modern permanent life insurance tools to today's smartphones. Not that long ago, you had a phone that was just a phone meant to make phone calls. You weren't surfing the internet, getting e-mails or text messages on your phone. Now, your phone does everything, including access the internet, take photos, function as a flashlight and GPS, and the list of its capabilities keeps growing every day. Well, the old insurance you are thinking about when you hear the words "life insurance" are like that old phone. Your old life insurance only had one purpose: to take care of your young family if you died prematurely. There were mortgages to pay and kids to put through school, so the goal was to get the maximum amount of death benefit for the least amount of money. Today's insurance, like the smartphone, has evolved over the last several years to meet the needs of the boomers. The primary benefits of many of today's life insurance policies include tax-free retirement income, long-term care benefits, and access to a tax-free emergency fund. It's worth taking a closer look.

Advanced Strategy

An advanced tax-reduction strategy involves combining a series of Roth IRA conversions with the build-up of a TLIF. This fund can be used to accomplish the following three extremely important goals:

1. provide tax-free income in retirement,

2. provide long-term care benefits, and

3. provide a tax-free lump sum death benefit.

Most people only think about the death benefit when they think about life insurance. And that certainly is a nice benefit to have. But did you know that you could have tax-free access to your life insurance during your lifetime? You can use that money for yourself to help fund your tax-free retirement. And the money you invest in this account will no longer be subject to market risk or tax rate risk. It can also be used to help offset health-care risk and provide additional financial security for your family.

This strategy has been utilized by the wealthy for years. When you hear about wealthy people who use advisors to help them find loopholes in the tax code to stay rich, this is one of the strategies they are talking about. Fortunately, these strategies are available to everyone. You just need to know about them.

Ed Slott, CPA, is a nationally recognized IRA-distribution expert, professional speaker, author, and creator of several public television specials. Slott was named the "best source for IRA advice" by the *Wall Street Journal* and called "America's IRA Expert" by *Mutual Funds Magazine*. In his *New York Times* best-selling books and in his PBS special, *Ed Slott's Retirement Roadmap*, Slott describes the tax-favored treatment of life insurance as the "biggest gift in the entire tax code." He says, "You [could be] moving large amounts of money from taxable accounts into a tax free permanent life insurance policy" that provides you with all these benefits.[18]

Everybody hates life insurance. But it's important to understand how you can use certain types of policies to generate tax-free income

18   Ed Slott, "ILU Tax Free Retirement," *Ed Slott's Road to Retirement.*

for you while you are alive. We are not talking about life insurance in the traditional sense, rather we are talking about the utilization of the tax-favored treatment of life insurance in the context of advanced tax reduction planning.

Think of this account as any other type of investment. All your accumulations are growing tax-free. With typical life insurance, you want the highest death benefit you can get for the lowest price. However, with this type of plan we are not as concerned with the death benefit as we are with the building of tax-free cash value. We specifically design this contract to maximize the accumulation of cash within the policy's cash account. We buy only as much death benefit as is required by the IRS, and put as much cash in the tax-free growth account as the IRS will allow. If you are approaching retirement, or have already retired and want to shelter as much as possible from future higher tax rates, then this may be a great tool for you.

The idea is to coordinate the use of Roth IRAs, tax-free life insurance, and other RMD elimination strategies so that your taxable income in retirement is as close to your deductions and exemptions as possible. By controlling your future taxable income, we may be able to help you reduce taxes on social security income and Medicare benefits, as well as taxes on ordinary income. The goal is for you to have more spendable income in your pocket.

The goal is for you to have more spendable income in your pocket.

Ideally, you could have let's say $100,000 of actual spendable income, but only have $20,000 of taxable income and $80,000 of tax-free income. You may also save on Social Security and Medicare taxes. Combining the savings on income, Social Security, and Medicare taxes alone could add up to many thousands of dollars in tax savings each and every year.

RMD ELIMINATION STRATEGY 3:
QUALIFYING LONGEVITY ANNUITY CONTRACT (QLAC)

In July 2014, the treasury department relaxed the RMD rules, reflecting the government's desire to encourage you to prepare financially for your retirement. The new rules allow you to buy a longevity annuity with your IRA money and not have to worry about including the value of that IRA Qualifying Longevity Annuity Contract in your RMD calculations from age seventy-and-a-half up to age eighty-five.

In 2014, a new tax rule became effective that allows people to utilize a portion of their tax-deferred plans to purchase a qualified longevity annuity contract (QLAC). These plans are exempt from RMD rules as long as the plan participant does not use more than 25 percent of their plan balance or $125,000 (whichever is less) to buy the longevity annuity.

For a couple, that means up to $250,000 could be placed into these QLACs, removing that money from the RMD calculations. They can defer RMDs on that $250,000 up until age eighty-five. For example, if there is a seventy-year-old couple, they can remove $250,000 from accounts used to calculate their required distributions. The result is a reduction of many thousands of dollars per year of fully taxable RMD income.

An important thing to know about QLACs is that they are available within 401(k), 403(b), Governmental 457, 401(a), and individual retirement accounts. Roth IRA accounts are not eligible. Inherited IRAs are not eligible. Accounts already in RMD are not eligible.

The funding vehicle for a QLAC will always be a special type of annuity called a longevity annuity. With this type of annuity, you pay a lump sum premium to an insurance company and then, at a future date, which you specify today (up to age eighty-five), you begin receiving a guaranteed monthly payout amount that continues for as long as you (or your spouse) are alive. The beauty of the longevity annuity is that the insurance company tells you today exactly how much income you will begin receiving in the future. There is no stock market or interest rate risk. The future income amount that's quoted is guaranteed. With a longevity annuity, you get income security that starts in your old age at an attractive price. Another appeal of QLACs is that they are straightforward and transparent. They are easy to understand, require only one upfront payment, and have no annual fees.

It's important to know that an annuity must be designed and labeled as a QLAC to qualify; just buying a longevity annuity is not enough. Longevity annuities have been around for years. But the way the IRS now treats a longevity annuity within a tax-deferred retirement account, such as an IRA or 401(k), has changed. Now each person can defer RMD on up to 25 percent of their account balances up to a maximum of $125,000. That $125,000 applies to all plans and IRAs collectively on an aggregated basis. If you have a plan with $100,000 in it, you can only take $25,000 out of that account (no more than 25 percent). But it can be up to $125,000, so you can take $25,000 from five different accounts. Income payments must begin no later than the first day of the month following the month of the participant's eighty-fifth birthday. Payments can be single or joint life—either life only or life with a cash refund. There are increasing payment options to help offset the impacts of inflation, and beneficiaries are guaranteed to get back 100 percent of contributions if you die prematurely.

Being able to avoid the RMD on $250,000 (as a couple) in retirement assets is a significant tax reduction tool. In addition, the guaranteed lifetime income provided by the longevity annuity may provide you and your family with protection against your major risk—longevity risk.

In summary, some of the more attractive features of the QLAC include:

- reduced taxes,

- decreased RMDs,

- planned future income,

- enhanced financial security for late retirement,

- protection of your savings from market downturns,

- no annual fees,

- deferred distributions,

- benefits to spouses and other beneficiaries,

- assisting strategies for leaving assets to heirs, and

- the potential for inflation protection.

RMD ELIMINATION STRATEGY 4:
NET UNREALIZED APPRECIATION (NUA) DISTRIBUTIONS

What is net unrealized appreciation? Some employees have the option to buy their company's stock within their 401(k)s or retirement plans. For example, Microsoft employees were able to buy their own company's stock as part of their retirement plan. For some, whether it's General Electric, Verizon, or whatever company it might be, the employees might have a big chunk of their 401(k) or retirement plan invested in their own company's stock. There are really no restrictions on the amount of company stock that you can hold in a plan. I often meet people who have almost all of their retirement money in company stock. If you have company stock in your retirement plan, when you retire and take a lump-sum distribution from your plan such as your 401(k), the distribution might include employer stock that is worth more than the fair market value at the time it was purchased in your account, so there may be a big appreciation in that approach.

The difference between the market value of your company's stock invested in your retirement plan at the time of the distribution and its value at the time your employer made the contribution to your plan is called *net unrealized appreciation* (NUA). For example, if the stock in your plan was purchased at $10 a share and it is now worth $100 a share, each share has $90 of NUA. The reason to care about this is because NUA receives extremely favorable tax treatment when distributed. And if the institution or advisor (if they even know about NUA) handling your rollover does not do it properly, it could cost you tens of thousands of dollars in unnecessary taxes. Unfortunately, I see people make this mistake all too often.

When you take a look at how NUA works, you have to understand that it only applies in two specific situations. First: If the stock shares are distributed in-kind as part of a lump-sum distribution, then 100 percent of the NUA is nontaxable at the time of distribution. You don't cash it out and have them send you cash. You actually have them send you the stock as part of the distribution.

Second: If the stock withdrawal is not a lump-sum distribution, then only the NUA attributable to your own contributions is nontaxable. If 100 percent of the stock in your plan was purchased through your payroll deductions, then you do not really have anything to worry about. But if you received stock from your employer as part of an incentive plan, you need to be careful that you follow the lump-sum distribution rules.

If you do have employer stock in your retirement plan, you need to be very careful to choose a new custodian who can actually accept the transfer of the new stock. The essence of the advantage of the

NUA is that the sales you make of company stock held in the non-IRA account you sent it to will be taxed at the capital gains rate rather than the ordinary income tax rates of traditional IRAs. And you get to control when you sell those shares of stock, and thus when you will pay the taxes.

Let's say you have company stock in your retirement plan and you retire and you are taking it out. If you roll that money completely into an IRA, when you take distributions from the IRA it's going to be taxed at the higher ordinary income tax rates. You can avoid paying these unnecessary taxes by asking your employer to send you the actual shares of stock—a stock certificate or a transfer of actual shares—and depositing the shares into a non-IRA after-tax account. Then, when you eventually sell the stock, you are going to pay capital gains tax rates on the distributions, as opposed to ordinary income tax rates.

Why is this so important? In 2017, if you are in the 15 percent tax bracket, capital gains rates are 0 percent. If you're in the 35 percent tax bracket, capital gains rates are 15 percent. And if you're in the 39.6 percent bracket, it's 20 percent. But 0 percent, 15 percent, or 20 percent beats 15 percent, 28 percent, or 33 percent any day. You could really save a bundle of money by taking advantage of net unrealized appreciation rules. Remember, this rule only applies to distributions of company stock.

In addition, the value of the shares you removed from your IRA, and all future growth on those dollars, will not be included in your RMD calculation at age seventy-and-a-half. Removing those dollars from your IRA could potentially save you thousands in taxes by excluding them from future RMD calculations.

Here's an example: Employee Jack retires and takes a lump-sum distribution of company stock worth $250,000. The money was contributed by the employer. Jack didn't put any money into it himself. If he takes that stock and puts it into a brokerage account instead of rolling it over to an IRA, and the company's cost basis is $50,000 in that account, the NUA is $200,000. Assuming he followed the lump-sum distribution rules properly, his NUA will not be taxed at the time of distribution. He will pay tax only on the original value of the stock at the time it was purchased in his plan. The amount Jack paid taxes on becomes his basis in the stock. He will not have to pay tax on the NUA portion until he sells the stock in a taxable account. When Jack eventually does sell the stock, he will get to pay tax at lower capital gains rates, instead of ordinary income tax rates.

As a huge bonus, when Jack turns seventy-and-a-half and must begin taking RMDs from his IRAs, the $250,000 he removed from his retirement plan, plus all future growth he may have earned on those dollars, will not be included in his RMD calculation. This strategy alone can save families tens of thousands of dollars of unnecessary taxes.

RMD ELIMINATION STRATEGY 5: QUALIFIED CHARITABLE DISTRIBUTION (QCD)

The Qualified Charitable Distribution (QCD) provision is one of the biggest tax breaks in the tax code and it is of tremendous value to those who are charitably inclined.

There are some retirees who have generous intentions. Some will even name a charity as a beneficiary or a partial beneficiary of their retirement plan. Others take RMD distributions from their IRAs, deposit the money in their bank account, and then write a check to their favorite charity or religious institution.

Instead of doing that, one thing retirees can do is take advantage of something called a Qualified Charitable Distribution. In 2006, Congress passed a law called the Pension Protection Act of 2006, that created the Qualified Charitable Distribution (QCD). QCD works particularly well for high-income earners. This law allows IRA owners to specify that a payment of up to $100,000 from their RMD be sent directly to a qualified charity. The owner electing this option is still required to take the RMD, but the amount of the distribution sent directly to the charity gets excluded from their gross income.

For people who are charitably inclined, a QCD can make a lot more sense than having the RMD sent to them, and then sending a separate check to the charity, particularly if the taxpayer can't itemize deductions. Many high-income earners (such as doctors, business owners, and other professionals) are subject to limitations on their total itemized deductions, including charitable contributions. So, if you can't itemize, the charitable contribution isn't tax deductible, and the IRA distribution is taxable. With the QCD, high-income earners still can't deduct the charitable donation, but they won't be taxed on the IRA distribution.

Other people may not be able to itemize deductions, because their home is paid off and they don't have enough medical and/or other expenses to make itemization possible. In this case, taxpayers are forced to take the standard deduction, meaning they cannot utilize the charitable contribution as a deduction on their tax return.

Take the case of Mr. and Mrs. Successful Couple. They are both professionals and high-income earners and feel fortunate to be living the American dream. They decided they would like to give back in the form of annual charitable contributions. They are both seventy-one, retired, and have large traditional IRAs. It is their intention this year to make a $10,000 donation to their favorite qualified charity, which is a foundation dedicated to fighting cancer in young adults. Because they are high-income earners, there are restrictions on their ability to itemize deductions. In addition, their charitable contributions cannot be deducted from their taxable income. Instead of taking their RMD as a taxable distribution and sending a check to the charity, they make the $10,000 contribution directly from their IRAs as a QCD, which is also enough to satisfy their RMDs. This strategy alone could reduce their taxable income by $10,000.

In addition, there are many other potential tax benefits from reducing your adjusted gross income using a QCD:

- less of your Social Security income may become taxable,

- the net investment income tax surcharge can be reduced, and

- you may avoid future increases in your Medicare premiums.

The Retirement Freedom Tax Plan helps you deal with the day of reckoning when you're going to have to start taking money out of your retirement plans. How much are you going to have to pay? You won't know until you need the money and you go to take it out. You are dealing with tax rate risk.

If you have a lot of tax deferred retirement money, you obviously have done a good job. You have saved a bunch of money in your 401(k), 403(b), and/or IRAs. Now you are facing a couple of risks including market risk—the risk of losing money in the markets and tax rate risk, the risk that future distributions will be subject to higher tax rates.

Utilizing the RMD reduction strategies outlined in this chapter, the Retirement Freedom Tax Plan can help you save thousands of dollars in taxes and keep substantially more of what you have earned. A penny saved is a penny earned and potentially saving tens of thousands of dollars in taxes will go a long way toward helping you live the retirement of your dreams. Now let's save you from going bankrupt should you get sick.

CHAPTER 4

Freedom to Remain in Your Own Home and Avoid Medicaid Bankruptcy

THE RETIREMENT FREEDOM LONG-TERM HEALTH-CARE PLAN

No retirement plan is complete without a plan for long-term care. Yet it is often overlooked, and for many seniors it is the only thing they have not planned for that could wipe out their entire life savings.

Long-term care has been referred to as the "million-dollar problem" that has no good solution for the American retiree. With life expectancies rising and costs for long-term care expected to rise in the coming decades, long-term care costs could represent $1 million or more in future liability for you and your family.

Stop and think about it for a minute: If your house burned down it would be a difficult time for you, but your insurance would pay for the move or help you rebuild. If you totaled your car, you may have some injuries, but the insurance company would protect you from lawsuits and replace your car. But what would happen if you needed full-time, around the clock care to help you live your life? What would that cost and how would you pay for it? How long would your savings last? What would happen to your spouse and family?

To provide a little perspective, American Association for Long-Term Care Insurance reports:[19]

- The odds of your home burning down between now and the day you die are approximately 3 percent, yet nearly every homeowner has homeowner's insurance.

- The odds of totaling your car between now and the time you die are about 18 percent, yet nearly every automobile owner carries auto insurance.

- The odds that you will need some form of long-term care between now and the day you die are about 72 percent. However, less than 30 percent of Americans over the age of forty-five have purchased long-term care insurance.

Long-term care is defined as the type of care given when someone needs assistance with their "activities of daily living" (ADL) due to an illness, accident, or old age. ADLs, or the activities of daily living, include bathing, dressing, continence, eating, using the toilet, and transferring (getting out of a bed, chair, car, and/or walking around).

This type of assistance can be given at home or in a facility. Long-term care is not one service, but many different services that provide people the help they need when a prolonged illness or disability keeps them from being able to do it themselves. It can range

---

19 "A Special Report on Long-Term Care Insurance Protection," American Association for Long-Term Care Insurance, 2010, https://www.aaltci.org/subpages/resources/claimsreport.pdf.

from help with day-to-day activities in the home to more sophisticated services, such as skilled nursing care in your home, in an assisted living facility, or as a last resort, in a nursing home.

While ADL describes the type of assistance needed, *skilled care* and *custodial care* are the most common terms used to define the level of care a person may require. Skilled care is generally necessary for medical conditions that require care from a physician, registered nurse, professional therapist, or other skilled medical professional. Skilled care is usually provided twenty-four hours a day, is ordered by a doctor, includes some type of treatment plan and is generally provided in a nursing home. It can also be provided in your home with visiting nurses and other health-care professionals.

Custodial care helps a person with their ADLs. It is less involved than skilled care, does not require a medical professional and can be performed at home, at adult daycare centers, at assisted living facilities, or at a nursing home.

It has been my experience that most people significantly underestimate the cost of long-term care. There are two different types of long-term care costs: First, there is the financial cost, but then, second, there is also the emotional cost of long-term care. These costs can literally tear families apart. It can ruin the health of the caregivers in the family and it can wipe out your savings. Consider these statistics:[20]

- The median private pay rate for a nursing facility in Massachusetts, for example, is $12,050 per month.

- The private pay rate for a Medicare-certified home health
- agency is $4,767 per month.

For our next case study, consider Joan, who has been retired for

---

20 "Cost of Care," Genworth Financial Inc, April 2016, https://www.genworth.com/aging-and-you/finances/cost-of-care.html.

many years now and finds herself in need of long-term care assistance. For now, a few hours a day from family members or adult daycare is adequate for her needs. However, as time goes by, Joan will require full-time care from a nursing home. Let's look at the potential costs: a year of care four hours per day, followed by a year of eight hours per day, followed by three years in a nursing home. Using today's costs, the total could be over $500,000, which leads to a couple questions. First, where is Joan going to get that money? And second, if this could you, what will your costs look like in fifteen or twenty years when you might need the same type of care? The only way you will have the money for this type of long-term care expense is to plan well in advance.

When you first need long-term care, your family will typically step in to provide that care, assuming, of course, they live anywhere near you. In many cases, families have relocated across the country, and extended families are not always available locally to help. However, most families will usually help if they can. They love you and want to take care of you. But you have to recognize the toll that providing this care will take on them. Being a caregiver is very expensive and can cause financial challenges. Your family will likely have to take time off from work and may have to spend their own money on many of the extras that you may need. They may also have to pay someone to be with you when they cannot be there.

And then there are the tremendous emotional challenges that caring for a loved one entails. Many people find themselves in the "sandwich generation," where they are not only caring for their children, but their parents as well. This role reversal of children taking care of their parents is very difficult emotionally. Balancing all of these priorities certainly increases the emotional and financial stressors on the caregiver.

Providing care can also be a physical challenge for most caregivers. Lifting someone into or out of bed or a bath tub, moving him or her from the living room to the kitchen, dressing and feeding a disabled family member, all takes a toll, especially if this is full time, twenty-four-seven care. Even if you can provide the time, taking care of someone twenty-four hours a day, seven days a week, will affect your life tremendously in many ways. Caregivers start out committing to taking care of a loved one, because it's just a few hours at first. But, looking down the road, it's not always going to be a few hours.

When you start out, you may be physically able to provide the care needed, but, over time, your back gives out, and then you are not able to move them at all. Caregivers can suffer hernias, back problems, or other physical problems. I know of a client who suffered a broken back taking care of her husband and ended up in a rehabilitation hospital herself for over six months. Then they have a problem, and you have a problem. It is a very slippery slope as you start out feeling good about doing it and you want to do it. But you don't consider that three years or five years from now for many reasons, you might not be able to do so anymore. Therefore, I say long-term care is not really about you; it is about your family. Since your family is on the front lines, consider what you can do to make their lives a little easier when it comes time to giving care.

> Long-term care is not really about you; it is about your family.

Medicare

Many people mistakenly believe that their health insurance or Medicare or some other government program is going to pay for their long-term care. The truth is that Medicare does not pay for most long-term care, and Medicaid will only pay once you have reached poverty levels—when all your money is gone. Personal health insurance and government programs will not cover the majority of long-term care costs. Health insurance covers medical costs such as tests, prescriptions, doctor visits, and hospitalizations. But it does not pay for long-term care costs. Government programs are restricted or limited when it comes to paying for long-term care. Medicare, for example, provides health insurance for people over age sixty-five, but it pays a small percentage of the overall long-term health-care costs nationally. It covers "acute care": care you would receive, say, from a doctor in a hospital. Medicare also pays for skilled care for medical professionals but does not pay for custodial care. And the truth is most people will actually end up needing custodial care, not skilled care, later in life.

In order to qualify for whatever care Medicare will cover, you have to have a three-day qualifying hospital stay, something that may or may not occur as you age naturally. Medicare will cover some home care under part B, but the services must be "medically necessary": a Medicare term that means supplies or services that are needed for a diagnosis or treatment of your medical condition. Medicare requires that a doctor must order home care services, and that you receive skilled treatment for an illness or injury. Help with bathing, dressing, eating, etc. are not considered medically necessary. They are considered custodial care and therefore are not usually covered.

Medicare also does not pay for room and board at an assisted living facility or adult day care. Again, Medicare covers only services that are considered "medically necessary" for the treatment of a specific medical condition. Even then Medicare will only pay for a maximum of one hundred days of nursing home care under Medicare part A, and then only if the three days or more of hospital stay has preceded the nursing home stay.

Finally, Medicare will only pay as long as you are showing progress in your rehabilitation. So, while Medicare will cover one hundred days in a nursing home after a three-day hospital stay, it will only cover those one hundred days if you are showing progress. The goal is that your stay in the nursing home must be assisting you to recover and lead to your return home. Once a condition stabilizes, Medicare benefits stop, even if you are still ill or not yet completely healthy.

I'm sure many of you reading this have had the unpleasant and often scary conversation with a social worker, case manager, and doctor at a nursing home or rehab where they are asking you what your plan is for Mom or Dad, because Medicare will no longer pay and your loved one needs to leave the facility.

So, it is important for people to understand that Medicare is not a program intended to cover long-term care needs. It is simply a health insurance program for those over age sixty-five. It does cover hospice and hospital care, but it is not designed to cover long-term care.

Medicaid

People often confuse Medicare and Medicaid. As we just discussed, Medicare does not pay for most long-term care, but will pay for a one-hundred-day stay in a nursing home (after a three-day hospital stay) as long as you continue to show improvement or make progress.

Medicaid, on the other hand, was created to provide health-care for people with low income and few assets. It is essentially a welfare program. Medicaid is often what people end up relying on to pay for long-term care expenses. For seniors, the Medicaid program offers both good news and bad news.

The good news is that Medicaid was developed to cover long-term care costs for Americans of any age who need help paying for those services. Medicaid currently pays about 45 percent of the national total spent on long-term care, primarily for nursing home facilities.

The bad news is that Medicaid is meant for people who are basically destitute. It is a form of welfare and requires a "means test."

To qualify for Medicaid, you first need to spend nearly all your savings before Medicaid will kick in. This is not what a lot of people had in mind when they began their retirement.

To be eligible for Medicaid, you need to meet specific medical and financial requirements. For instance, if you are single, you are only allowed to have $2,000 in "countable" assets in your name. "Countable" assets generally include all your belongings except for personal possessions such as clothing, furniture, jewelry, one motor vehicle (valued up to $4,500 for unmarried recipients and of any value for community spouses), your principal residence, and any assets that are considered inaccessible for one reason or another (e.g., a properly drafted irrevocable trust that was set up at least five years prior to the Medicaid need). All other assets above the limit are considered "countable," including your IRA, 401(k), investment portfolio, second home, and more. As of 2017, if you are married and your spouse plans to continue living in the community, they are allowed to keep a maximum of $109,560 in their name. If you apply with more assets than this, you will be required to spend those assets down before qualifying for coverage.

Obviously, these asset limits put families in the difficult position of either being denied Medicaid eligibility or having to spend most of their hard-earned assets on health-care costs, leaving nothing for their families, and potentially leaving their spouse with little resources to survive.

Another barrier to achieving Medicaid eligibility is the five-year look-back period. The Division of Medical Assistance (DMA) has the right to examine your bank and financial records for up to five years when reviewing your application. If the DMA discovers a transfer of assets during this period, they will impose a disqualification period on your eligibility. The length of disqualification period (in months) is determined by dividing the amount transferred by approximately $8,000 (the monthly cost of privately paid Medicaid). For example, a transfer of $80,000 would result in a ten-month disqualification period, starting when the applicant is otherwise qualified for Medicaid. This disqualification period can have devastating effects on your financial estate.

To add insult to injury, if you do end up on Medicaid, there is a process known as "estate recovery" where Medicaid can recoup money that they spent for your care from your estate after your death. What this means is that even though your primary residence was not in jeopardy while you were living, at your death your primary residence could be sold, and the proceeds go to the state instead of your family.

If this seems unfair or harsh, remember that Medicaid is a program that was established to help poor people have access to health-care and retain some dignity as they age. It was never meant for people who want to remain at home, or for people who want to protect their assets to pass them along to their family.

If the government requires you to spend your assets before they will pay for your long-term care, what other options do you have if you don't want to have to go down that road?

Limited Options

The bottom line is there are basically only three ways to pay for long-term care:

1. Pay for long-term care out of your own pocket.

2. Try to qualify for Medicaid once you are destitute.

3. Transfer the risk to an insurance company and they will help pay for your long-term care should you need it.

SO, HOW DO YOU PAY FOR LONG-TERM CARE?

The first option is to self-fund. Self-funding simply means that you will pay all of the expenses for your care with your personal savings and assets, at least until you spend down enough to qualify for Medicaid. This happens to be one of the most popular options, because if you have not made a plan for your long-term care, the government has established this plan for you. You might not like this plan, but it is the default option for people who don't have any plan at all—that's the plan they're on whether they realize it or not. The plan is: spend all your own money till you are destitute and then Medicaid will cover the rest.

Is that your best option? I don't think so. Take a step back and review your life so far. You probably have a home and a couple of cars. You have a 401(k), maybe an IRA, and some type of brokerage and savings account. You may own some CDs, some annuities, and some life insurance. Perhaps you have a second home or a condo. You have been trying to build your wealth and at the same time protect yourself from large-scale disasters. You have homeowner's insurance, automobile insurance, and you probably have disability insurance if you're working. These are all prudent ways to handle risk. However, at retirement, some of these protections disappear.

Maybe you lose the group life insurance and the disability insurance that you had at work. Your other term life insurance policies might be too expensive to keep. Your income may change from a bi-monthly paycheck to a monthly annuity or Social Security and pension. But if you are forced into some type of Medicaid spend-down, all those things that you tried to plan for and cover—your income and your assets—are all going to be put in jeopardy by redirecting that money for your long-term care.

If you develop some type of medical condition and require

long-term care, you can certainly start by using your current income, but given the costs and the length that might be needed, the reality is you're probably not going to have enough. At that point, you begin dipping into your principal and pretty soon your assets are generating less and less income as you dig deeper into principal. Not only does your retirement savings get blown through, your ability to generate income is also gone.

You could take a chance that you might not need long-term care, but the odds are against you. About 70 percent of Americans over age sixty-five will need some form of long-term care services at some point in their lives. This doesn't necessarily mean in a nursing home, but some type of home health-care or assisted living situation for either a short, immediate period, or for the long-term. People are living longer and longer but they're not necessarily physically or mentally healthy all that time. If you don't have any type of long-term care plan, you're really taking a gamble.[21]

I have found for most people the best funding option is some type of long-term care (LTC) insurance. LTC insurance can work in conjunction with your Medicare plan. When you have a good LTC insurance policy, it will cover services across the spectrum of care, including home care, adult day care, assisted living facilities, residential care facilities, nursing homes, and even hospice care.

LTC insurance also addresses some of the limitations we discussed earlier. There is no hospital stay requirement for example, and there is no income or asset means test to pass. You simply need what are called the "benefit triggers" (which are identified in your policy), and then you must satisfy what is called the "elimination period."

The benefit triggers are generally the inability to perform activi-

---

21   "The Basics," LongTermCare.gov, last updated October 10, 2017, accessed September 2018, https://longtermcare.acl.gov/the-basics/.

ties, or two out of five ADLs. Your doctor must certify that you can no longer perform these activities, triggering a benefit. Some type of cognitive impairment or dementia would also trigger a benefit. The trigger can be a physical or mental impairment and then benefits begin at the end of the elimination period.

An elimination period is a bit like the deductible where you pay for the first, second, or third month out of pocket, and then the long-term care policy kicks in. It is a way to keep your premiums lower. The longer the elimination period, the more affordable the policy will be. If you think about it, not only does long-term care insurance benefit the person listed on the policy, but it could also help protect the entire family. Financially speaking, it allows you to spend money on what you want to spend it on rather than what you have to spend it on. And it could leave your retirement and estate plan strategies intact. You could have the best retirement plan and the best estate plan in place, but a long-term care need could come along and devastate both of those plans if you are not prepared.

Emotionally, long-term care insurance provides you with available resources like the guidance of a care coordinator who can allow your family to be with you while you are receiving care, rather than be the ones administering the care. Long-term care insurance can also help you stay in your home longer. If you have home health-care, adult day care, and assisted living coverage, that may allow you to hopefully stay in your home longer. In fact, I have come to look at long-term care coverage as a "keep me out of the nursing home" policy.

How do you sort through all the information? How do you find the best policy for you? When you are shopping for long-term care insurance, there are a few things you want to look at. One, you want to start by looking at the company itself. Look for high financial ratings and a history of integrity. You may not need this policy for twenty or thirty years. You want to make sure that the company is reliable and is still going to be there when you need it. So first up, look for a good strong company with excellent financial strength and stability.

You also want to look for a comprehensive policy that offers a wide range of benefits, because everyone's needs could be a little bit different at the time of a claim. One feature in the policy to look for is the length of coverage. It could be three years, five years, seven years, or it could be a lifetime policy. Some policies will pay out the benefits for five years and then stop, whereas others will pay for a lifetime. Of course, the policy that is going to pay for five years is going to be less expensive than the policy that is going to pay forever.

When you consider the type of coverage, you also want to make sure the policy has some type of home health-care coverage. Check the daily benefit rates. Is it $100, is it $150, or is it $200? Usually when you buy long-term care insurance, you are buying a daily benefit, so study what the expenses are in your area for the cost of care and buy your policy accordingly. Another thing to bear in mind here is that, generally, you're not buying long-term care insurance to cover 100 percent of the expense. If you have a nursing home that costs $100,000 a year and you have a long-term care policy that can pay $50,000 to 70,000 a year, that benefit amount may be adequate to protect your assets. Think of it as offsetting the expense.

Depending on your age, you might want a policy where the payments are inflation adjusted. If you start out at $200 a day, does it stay at $200 a day, or does it go up? You could buy a policy when you're fifty years old and it starts at $200 a day, but it goes up every year. By the time you actually file a claim, perhaps it is paying $300 a day, helping you keep pace with inflation.

A LTC policy with an inflation rider will be more expensive, which is why you have to consider all the policy features and what they offer, figuring out what benefits you actually want/need and what you can afford. Then buy the policy accordingly.

If you are married, you must consider how your long-term care needs will affect your spouse. For those without insurance coverage, a spouse may be forced to pay for a caregiver from their own savings. It could create a financial burden, and leave minimal remaining assets for the spouse to enjoy their own financial security. An unanticipated long-term care event can literally wipe out an entire life savings. Long-term care insurance helps to protect assets from the cost of an expensive illness, and thus protect a healthy spouse in the process.

Another benefit of long-term care insurance is the removal of the caregiver burden for family members. Instead of enduring the mental and physical stress that providing care can create, your family can spend their time with you instead of taking care of you. If you are single and don't have a spouse or close relative nearby to help take care of you, long-term care insurance can provide you with reassurance that your needs are going to be taken care of as you age. Long-term care insurance can coordinate the care you need, as well as help pay for it, giving you peace of mind.

According to the American Association for Long-Term Care Insurance, claims on long-term care policies break down like this: 43 percent are for home health-care, 30 percent are for assisted living and only 25 percent are for nursing homes. So, 75 percent of the benefits are paid out to people who are getting care in their home or an assisted living facility.[22]

---

22 "Long-Term Care Insurance Facts – Statistics," American Association for Long-Term Care Insurance, accessed September 2018, http://www.aaltci.org/long-term-care-insurance/learning-center/fast-facts.php.

What determines the cost of a long-term care policy? The cost of your long-term care policy is based on:

- how old you are when you buy the policy;

- the maximum amount that a policy will pay per day;

- the maximum number of days/years that a policy will pay;

- whether you have inflation protection or not; and

- the maximum amount per day multiplied by the number of days, which determines the lifetime maximum amount that the policy will pay.

Another factor to consider is your health. Any type of health issue or medical condition could affect the cost of your premium. And a traditional long-term care insurance policy works just like a homeowner's policy: you renew it every year. However, you only have to qualify medically at the initial application.

If you are in poor health or already receiving long-term care services, you may not qualify for long-term care insurance as most individual policies require medical underwriting. In some cases, you may be able to buy a limited amount of coverage, or coverage at a higher "non-standard" rate. Some group policies do not require underwriting.

One concern people have with LTC insurance is that they may never use the benefit. There are provisions in some traditional policies that include a money back guarantee. If the policyholder never uses the long-term care benefit, the premium can be reverted to the family later on. The refund usually comes in the form of a death benefit. This helps overcome the one objection that some people have to long-term care insurance: the concern that if they don't need the coverage they have just wasted their money on unnecessary insurance premiums.

New Option: Hybrid LTC Policies

Hybrid LTC policies: a solution to the problem of wasted premiums.

Unlike traditional LTC policies that have a premium "pay-as-you-go" approach, hybrid policies link your LTC benefit to a life insurance policy. These types of policies are usually funded with a one-time single premium up-front payment such as $50,000 or $100,000. In return, the insurance company provides the contract owner a tax-free death benefit and access to the death benefit proceeds during lifetime to help pay for qualifying long-term care expenses.

The appeal of hybrid LTC life insurance policies is that you or your family are guaranteed to receive your cash back should you never need to receive long term care. In fact, your beneficiaries could receive many times the amount you paid in premiums.

Many hybrid long-term care insurance policies will:

- pay for your costs up to the limits of your policy should you need care,

- provide your estate with a tax-free life insurance benefit should you not need care, and

- offer you a money-back guarantee should you change your mind.

For example, consider the sixty-year-old Betsy. She has already set aside $500,000 in her savings for future expenses including long-term care. As an alternative to self-funding her LTC needs, she could choose to move $200,000 of the $500,000 in her savings account into a linked-benefit hybrid life insurance policy. In doing so, depending on the type of policy she is purchasing, her coverage may look something like this:

- $400,000 of long term care benefits ($8,100 month for fifty months) covering home health-care, assisted living or nursing home care,

- a tax-free death benefit to her family if she never needs the care, and

- access to cash value.

Hybrid insurance policies may be worth considering if you have liquid assets not needed for retirement income that can be repositioned, or if you have RMD payments that are currently being deposited in the bank or put at risk in the market and could be put to better use to help solve LTC risk.

The main benefit of having long-term care coverage, in my opinion, is the idea that the insurance may help keep you in your own home for as long as possible. With adequate home health-care and assisted living benefits, a good long-term care insurance policy can help keep you out of the nursing home.

I can't stress enough that no retirement plan is complete without a plan for long-term care. These plans provide help with the physical and emotional stress for family members who are providing the care. If you end up paying for long-term care out of pocket it's a physical, emotional, and financial strain on both you and your family.

Long-term care benefits give the control back to you. Most importantly, you're more likely to be able to stay in your own home and out of a nursing home with a proper plan. In addition, your family will be relieved of some of the financial, physical, and emotional burden of your care. An effective long-term care strategy is one of the best gifts you can give your spouse and family. With a long-term care plan, you've not only bought control over your health-care needs, you've bought peace of mind. Now let's tackle your estate plan.

CHAPTER 5

Freedom to Build a Legacy and Be Remembered

★ ★ ★

THE RETIREMENT FREEDOM LEGACY OPTIMIZATION PLAN

★ ★ ★

The Retirement Freedom Estate Plan is a combination of trust and tax planning that seeks to minimize taxes and burdens to your family, while also maximizing the transfer of your wealth to your children, grandchildren, and/or favorite charitable organizations.

Many people are worried about the future financial security of their children and grandchildren. To be fair, many people I speak with are more concerned about the future well-being of their grandchildren. They talk about the enormous federal debt we will be leaving behind and how that debt may affect their loved ones' ability to achieve financial security in the future. People also feel the world seems to be spinning more and more out of control every day, and would like to be able to help protect future generations of their family.

Building an effective estate plan, including advanced legacy strategies, is a great way to take care of your family after you are gone. It is also a wonderful way to be remembered for generations to come as the thoughtful, loving, and caring person you are.

What kind of legacy do you want to leave behind? Will you leave chaos? Or will you leave a well-conceived plan with information and resources to help your family when they need it the most? The choice is yours.

Estate Planning

The primary goal of estate planning should be to protect and preserve your family in the event of your incapacity or death. Estate planning is not only about the use of wills, trusts, and other documents; it is also about utilizing advanced legacy strategies to leverage what you have.

Many clients are reluctant to discuss death and disability, especially with family members, so frequently families are left in the dark. For example, how many children know where their parents want to be buried? Or who the pallbearers should be? Today, many people have their pertinent information stored on their computer. Even if their documents are in order in there, they don't realize that nobody has the passwords they would need to access them. What happens when your children can't find the password to your computer? They can't manage your affairs.

There are many things you can do while you are alive to help protect and preserve your family. You may think you are going to be well enough to tell your children what you want, or where the important papers are filed, but the truth is you may not be. You may be incapacitated. Or you may die suddenly before you get the chance to convey that information. The last thing you want is for your loved ones to try and guess your desires when they are grieving your passing.

Over 70 percent of Americans do not have even a basic estate plan. Failure to have a plan, and the subsequent failure to provide this basic information, may create family conflicts at a difficult time. It can also cause the dissipation of assets you spent a lifetime building. It could result in the payment of income and estate taxes that could have been avoided. But primarily it could cause a lot of stress and pain for the family you are leaving behind. Your incapacity or death is already going to be a traumatic event for them. The mental fogginess that accompanies a family's trauma is exaggerated by their inability to make rudimentary decisions due to a lack of information.

Every estate plan should consist of at least these three elements: (1) a plan designed to provide for the disposition of your assets in the manner you desire, (2) the proper execution of documents that fully provide for your incapacity and death, and (3) detailed facts about your assets and liabilities. I recommend that everyone consider each of the following documents as part of their basic estate plan.

THE FAMILY LOVE LETTER

One of the most important documents that you can put together for your family is something I like to call the family "love letter." This document provides instructions for the family regarding your intentions, wishes, and where they can find things.

My recommendation is that you complete the family love letter as a document. Keep a copy with your important records, and maybe provide a copy to either family members or their advisers. I also recommend calling a family meeting with advisers and beneficiaries where you can discuss the document, and make sure your family is using some type of roadmap to know exactly what your wishes and desires are. This is just one part of a larger estate plan, but it's a very important one that is often overlooked.

A WILL

A will is a document that is written for the probate court. It provides instructions to the judge on how you want to dispose of your assets. Your will is your final declaration of how your assets should be treated after your death. This document needs to be thought out carefully and should deal with all of the potential issues that may face your survivors.

Many people want simple wills, but fail to realize the importance of the well-drafted will. People are going online these days to use self-service websites (fill out your will for a hundred bucks in five minutes and you're all set). If you don't really have any assets, or minor children, then maybe that's an okay decision. But most of the families I work with have fairly significant assets they would like to protect. Some also have charitable intentions. They have surviving spouses. They have children and grandchildren they want to take care of. Therefore, it's very important that even a simple will be well thought out.

Your will has a number of purposes including detailing how your assets should be disposed of at your death and choosing the right people to make decisions when you are gone. Sometimes you will need to create trusts for heirs who may lack the maturity or talent to manage inherited assets. You may also wish to provide for the guardianship of any minor children, minimize estate taxes, reduce state and federal income taxes, and lessen the source of potential conflicts among your family members.

It's important to realize that the failure to have an estate plan, including a well-drafted will, can result in significant problems. For example, a deceased husband with no will and two children from a prior marriage may be able to convey only 33 percent of his estate to his surviving wife. If instructions were not established by a will, children from a prior marriage may be entitled to receive those assets.

The court will also decide how to manage the money you may have left for any minor children. If you leave them money and they're not yet eighteen years old, they can't manage it legally on their own. Somebody will be appointed by the court to determine how those dollars are going to be spent, and it might not be the way you planned.

As you can see, failure to have a will can cause serious confusion, difficulty, and problems for your family. That's why it's very important to have that will well thought out and executed.

A LIVING WILL

Another document that should be part of your estate plan is a living will. A living will is a declaration that you do not desire life-sustaining treatment if there is no significant hope of your recovery in the event of an illness. For example, if you want to be taken off life support, including intravenous nourishment and fluids, you must have declared your desire for this before becoming incapacitated.

It's never too early to have a living will, and failure to have a medical directive upon incapacity can create tremendous emotional stress for your family. Again, writing this document and doing this planning for your family is an expression of love for your family. It's truly a gift.

A REVOCABLE LIVING TRUST

Another document you might want to consider is a revocable living trust. Often what people will do to maintain control of their assets at incapacity or death is to put certain assets into a revocable living trust.

A revocable living trust is a legal agreement under which the trustee manages certain assets for your benefit or for the benefit of others during your lifetime and after your death. Should you become incapable of handling your own personal finances, for example, the living trust can pay your medical bills and living expenses. And since assets in a living trust avoid probate at your death, your family may save many thousands of dollars in probate fees, expenses, and delays. In addition, since a living trust is a private agreement, information concerning the contents of it remains private.

You can modify the terms of a living trust, change beneficiaries, or terminate the trust as your goals change. And you can elect to have the trust cease following your death, or continue on for your beneficiaries.

A word of caution regarding revocable living trusts: Unless you have a testamentary trust that is funded at death through a provision in your will, you must make sure to *retitle your assets into the name of the trust.* This includes real estate, bank accounts, brokerage accounts, and other assets. If you neglect to finalize the trust funding process by retitling your assets, you may find the trust does not do you any good.

The Potential Problems of Joint Ownership

Another reason to consider a revocable living trust is to avoid some of the potential pitfalls of joint ownership. Often, people have lots of their assets owned jointly, which can potentially cause a lot of challenges.

When you own something jointly with somebody, the moment one of the owners passes away, the assets then become 100 percent owned by the surviving joint owner. You might own all kinds of different assets jointly, such as real estate, bank accounts, brokerage accounts, etc. Second marriages without specific estate documents and written intentions can be tough on families, too. You own everything jointly with your second spouse, and then you pass away. All your jointly-owned assets immediately become 100 percent owned by the surviving spouse who may intentionally or even unintentionally disinherit your children from your first marriage.

Another issue with joint ownership can arise when you name children as joint owners on your bank account or real estate. What you may not realize is that an adult child on the title to your home can successfully get sued. Maybe they're in the process of a divorce. Maybe they owe money to the IRS. In these events, you could potentially lose your home. The joint owner has every right to transfer their share, 50 percent of that asset, to anyone else they want at any time without your knowledge or approval. Or if your co-owner becomes incapacitated, you could find yourself a new co-owner—the court.

A MEDICAL POWER OF ATTORNEY

A medical power of attorney is another document that is necessary. While a living will is simply a declaration not to use life-sustaining measures, a medical power attorney is designated to grant someone the power to make medical decisions upon your incapacity. I generally recommend signing both a medical power of attorney and a living will. Having a medical power attorney helps assure your family members, and not your doctors, have the final say in your treatment. If it's clear that life cannot be sustained, the power holder can step away and allow the living will to take effect.

A discussion of these documents is important to have with your family because sometimes people—without really thinking too much about it—will name one of the children as their health-care proxy or medical power of attorney. Often that puts tremendous strain and sometimes guilt on the child or family member who has to make these life or death decisions. If you've written it down in advance, and you have discussed it with your children, then everybody will know your intentions and wishes. This is helpful to whoever may be left to make those difficult decisions.

A DURABLE GENERAL POWER OF ATTORNEY

You also want to have a durable general power of attorney document, which provides the legal power to a person you name in the document to act on your behalf and manage your assets if you become incapacitated. In some states, such a document must state specifically that it survives you at incapacity, and in other states the document can be drafted so it's not triggered until you become incapacitated, so it's always wise to make sure the language is correct in the document. If it is not the right type of power of attorney with the right language, the power of attorney can be revoked, perhaps at exactly the time that you most need it. Some people worry about losing control while they are alive.

These documents should be drafted with extraordinary detail to assure that the power holder maintains as much authority as possible. A short document with minimal detail that grants all authority to your power holder can create significant restrictions to the power holder in making decisions, e.g., in handling tax issues.

A PERSONAL PROPERTY DISPOSITION LIST

Another document you should have is a personal property disposition list. It's critically important. I see more family conflicts over insubstantial personal property than over any other issue. Ask your children in advance what assets they might want when you are gone. Then prepare your detailed list, perhaps even with pictures, directing how these assets should be passed on.

If your children or grandchildren are too young, use a list to describe which assets and family heirlooms you want your personal representative to hold for them until they are more mature. If you are married, you should consider preparing a list describing which assets belong to you, and which assets belong to your spouse, especially if there are children from a prior marriage.

To summarize, the documents in the basic estate-planning checklist include a will or living trust or both, a living will, a medical power of attorney, a general power of attorney, a personal property disposition list, and the family love letter. A qualified estate planning professional should be consulted to see what documents are appropriate for your unique situation and goals.

The Importance of Beneficiary Designations

Another critically important document to review regarding your estate plan is your named beneficiary designations on retirement plans, insurance, and annuities. One of the most common mistakes people make is naming the wrong beneficiaries on life insurance policies, annuities, IRAs, and 401(k)s. They often don't realize that retirement plans, such as IRAs, 403(b)s, 401(k)s, as well as life insurance policies and annuity policies do not go through your will. They also don't go through a trust unless you have named a trust as beneficiary.

Whoever you have named as beneficiary on your retirement plan documents is who will receive the money, regardless of what your will or other legal documents say. Sometimes these beneficiary designations were made many years ago. You might not even remember whom you named as beneficiary, or previous designations may no longer be valid because of changes in your will or family circumstances. Have you taken your ex-spouse off your IRA, 401(k), and life insurance as beneficiary? If not, this can be a real problem.

For example, George and Susan live in New York. They met much later in life, fell in love, and got married. It was the first marriage for Susan. She had worked in the retirement system for the State of New York for thirty-five years and had accumulated over one million dollars in her 403(b) retirement plan.

When Susan set up that plan initially, she had named her sister as her beneficiary. It would be many years before Susan would meet and marry George, and she never thought to change who her beneficiary was listed as. When Susan passed away, George assumed he would inherit his wife's 403(b) money.

When it came time to distribute Susan's assets, her sister ended up getting all of Susan's money. George fought this in court, but he lost. The sister was the legal beneficiary on the account. Susan didn't realize it, but she had disinherited her husband by not changing the beneficiary designation on her retirement plan when she married George.

> Every few years, you should obtain written confirmation of your life insurance, retirement plan, and annuity beneficiary designations.

Every few years, you should obtain written confirmation of your life insurance, retirement plan, and annuity beneficiary designations. You don't want to designate minor children as beneficiaries, even as contingent beneficiaries, because if they inherit the assets prior to age eighteen, those assets will have to be managed by the court who will have to name a conservator of those assets.

If you have minor children whom you do want to inherit some of your money, it may make sense to set up a trust as beneficiary where the assets can be held until your heirs have reached sufficient maturity to handle the money, usually eighteen years of age. Such a trust needs to have special language included or distributions from the retirement plan could be accelerated, causing an increase in taxes and loss of valuable tax-deferral. You want to be very careful when naming a trust as beneficiary of a retirement plan, so be sure to get some professional help.

The Legacy Optimization Plan

You can help protect your children and grandchildren from the economic uncertainties of the future. Grandparents of today are in a unique position to make the most of what they've got. They can begin by leveraging their retirement plans and gifting their RMDs to a life insurance policy that will help protect their family.

You can leverage your IRA by using the one of the biggest benefits in the tax law: the tax exemption for life insurance. The absolute best time to do this with your IRAs is in your sixties. Specifically, I mean between the ages of fifty-nine-and-a-half and seventy-and-a-half when there are fewer IRA tax rules and no deadlines. You can't take out too much and you can't take out too little. You can't take it out too early and you can't take it out too late.

Remember, with a traditional IRA you will get hit with a 10 percent penalty for taking your money out before turning fifty-nine-and-a-half, and after turning seventy-and-a-half you'll get hit with a 50 percent penalty for not taking out enough. Between the ages of fifty-nine-and-a-half and seventy-and-a-half, you have complete flexibility to withdraw penalty-free and leverage your IRA using the tax-exemption and invest in life insurance.

The idea is to take one's RMD payment each year and *gift* the proceeds to a permanent life insurance policy. Instead of taking the money from your RMD and putting it in the bank at 1 percent, or investing the money in the stock market where it could be lost, why not send the RMD to the insurance company, thereby setting your family up with a lump-sum tax-free death benefit? These tax-free funds can be used to protect the financial future of your loved ones and potentially provide them opportunities they may not otherwise have had. This strategy utilizes the smart use of leverage with your retirement dollars.

Of course, it depends on your age, health, and other factors, but it could be that for every dollar you invest in your life insurance, your family could be paid many multiples of that amount tax-free at your death.

Let's take a look at Bob. He is sixty-four years old and has a large IRA with a balance of nearly $750,000. Since Bob has a pension and other resources, he doesn't really need the money from his IRA to live on. However, he knows that when his RMDs start, he will be receiving $25,000 to $30,000 each year whether he wants the money or not. He's not happy about paying taxes on those distributions, and worries that tax rates may go up in the future. He has decided to take our advice and start taking money out of his IRA now to avoid future tax rate risk.

Bob decides to gift $25,000 per year into a permanent life insurance policy and name his spouse, children, and grandchildren as beneficiaries. As a result, when Bob passes, his family will receive a tax-free windfall of well over $1 million. Of course, they will also receive whatever is left in his IRA. Bob has turned a fully taxable $750,000 (perhaps $400,000 net after taxes) account into a $1 million tax-free account, plus the money remaining in his IRA.

Think of the leverage Bob was able to achieve with his IRA. He was able to provide his family tax-free cash when they will need it the most. This money will now be available to help his spouse with added financial security, as well as his children and grandchildren with education expenses or whatever else they need for financial security in the future. Bob has helped build a financial fortress around his family to protect them in the future when he is no longer there to protect them himself.

Advanced Strategy: Tax-Free Roth Conversion Strategy

For the previous example, an advanced legacy planning strategy would be for Bob's beneficiaries to take some of the tax-free cash they receive from the life insurance policy and use it to pay the taxes on a Roth IRA conversion. Now, in addition to the tax-free life insurance benefit, they will also be able to receive a lifetime of tax-free distributions from their inherited IRAs. This strategy is extremely powerful and can result in hundreds of thousands of additional tax-free income for your heirs.

What if you end up needing the money during your lifetime? If structured properly, you can pull out your cash value tax-free to help with your own expenses.

The basic purpose of life insurance is to create cash—nothing more, nothing less. Everything else just confuses and complicates the issue of life insurance. It's an instrument anyone can use to leverage pennies into dollars. In my opinion, this combination of leverage and the incredible tax breaks given to life insurance makes it an extremely powerful and effective way to transfer large amounts of tax-free cash to your children and grandchildren.

This combination of leverage and the incredible tax breaks given to life insurance makes it an extremely powerful and effective way to transfer large amounts of tax-free cash to your children and grandchildren.

If you don't need your RMDs to live on, then consider gifting them to a life insurance policy with your loved ones as beneficiaries. Where else can you put those dollars and receive that type of internal rate of return on a tax-free basis? Nowhere!

Through the proper use of legal documents, life insurance, and detailed letters of instruction to your family, you can rest assured you have done everything possible to protect your family in the event of your incapacitation or passing. I can think of no greater expression of love than to take the time to put together a comprehensive estate and legacy optimization plan for the people you love. The Retirement Freedom Estate and Legacy Optimization Plan is a great way to accomplish this.

Conclusion

In case you haven't noticed, there's a common theme throughout this book. That's right: freedom. The term "financial freedom"—more specifically, "retirement freedom"—gets used quite often. But what exactly does "freedom" mean?

We've gone over freedom from fear, freedom from the Wall Street behemoths, and freedom from nursing homes, as well as the freedom to keep your money, and the freedom to make a difference. In short, retirement freedom is the self-sustained ability to keep the things you don't like at bay, and the ability to partake in the things you enjoy. Doesn't sound so bad, does it? It's actually an amazing concept, and one that I have seen bring joy to people for nearly three decades. But don't just take my word for it.

Study after study shows that people who have a comprehensive retirement and estate plan feel happier and more secure than those who do not. More than eight in ten people who work with financial professionals believe they are better prepared for retirement as a result of that relationship, and it's only common sense that those who have a written plan for retirement are not only in a better place financially, but they also have a more positive outlook about their retirement future than those who do not have a plan.[23]

Overall happiness, well-being, and self-esteem are influenced more by our sense of financial control than by how much we deposit in the bank every month. A comprehensive, well-defined retirement plan not only benefits you when you start making withdrawals, but it can also improve your quality of life immediately with a boost in confidence by eliminating the fear of future financial insecurity. That's an immediate return on investment I'll take any day.

Gaining control of your financial situation is the primary objective of the Retirement Freedom Solution. I believe maintaining financial control is the key to happiness and peace in retirement, regardless of how much money you have in the bank.

I often ask people "Have you done all the things that you wanted to do in retirement? Did you join the country club, buy a new boat, go on a cruise, or see the world?" Too many times the answer is, "No."

Why? Because they need to keep their money, "Just in case." Well, guess what happens to that "just in case" money? It often goes to the kids—who join the country club, buy the boat, and see the world. I want all my clients to have a wonderful and exciting retirement; I don't want them to live a "just in case" retirement. The Tax and Investment Advisors Retirement Freedom Solution will help you stop worrying about money and do just that.

I have used my experience in the financial world to develop this exclusive program. It was specifically engineered to help current and future retirees simplify their financial life, reduce taxes, manage risk, and generate consistent cash flow. More importantly, by implement-

---

23 Insured Retirement Institute, *Boomer Expectations for Retirement 2016: Sixth Annual Update on the Retirement Preparedness of the Boomer Generation*, April 2016, accessed September 2018, https://www.myirionline.org/docs/default-source/research/boomer-expectations-for-retirement-2016.pdf.

ing the ideas in this book, you will gain the confidence needed to enjoy retirement to the fullest.

Now, let's make it work for you, because you deserve it.

ABOUT THE AUTHOR
Robert A. Guy, RICP®

Author, speaker, educator and advocate for his clients, Robert A. Guy, RICP® has been helping families turn their lifetimes of work into the retirement they deserve for more than twenty-five years. He has dedicated his career to providing unbiased advice and sophisticated strategies to people who want to enjoy retirement to the fullest. His professional mission is to help families secure a long and comfortable retirement with no reduction in lifestyle and no real fear of running out of money.

Rob graduated from the University of Massachusetts at Amherst in 1988 with a bachelor of science degree in finance and began his career with American Express Financial Advisors. Feeling he could better serve his clients as an independent financial advisor, Rob established his own firm in 1992. He has devoted nearly thirty years committed to helping hundreds of Boston-area families work toward getting the most from their retirement dollars and enjoying the worry-free retirement they deserve.

Rob specializes in cutting-edge tax reduction techniques, advanced social security and pension maximization strategies, evidence-based wealth management, effective asset protection methods, and thoughtfully crafted estate and wealth transfer plans.

Rob holds several federal and state licenses including the Series 7, 24, 63, and 65. Robert has also earned his Retirement Income Certified Professional designation from the American College of Financial Services in Bryn Mawr, Pennsylvania. He offers fee-based investment and financial planning advice to clients while adhering to the Fiduciary Standard, ensuring that clients are receiving unbiased advice in their best interest.

When not at work helping his clients plan for a more secure retirement, you can usually find Rob with his better half, Jen, spending time near the ocean with family and friends.

Printed in the USA
CPSIA information can be obtained
at www.ICGtesting.com
JSHW012040140824
68134JS00033B/3174

9 781599 324241